The Immigrant's Guide to the American Workplace

Making It in America

Anna Graf Williams
Daljinder Kooner
Mary Jo Dolasinski
Karen J. Hall

Upper Saddle River, NJ 07458

Library of Congress Cataloging-in-Publication Data

The immigrant's guide to the American workplace: making it in America / Anna Graf Williams . . . [et al.].
   p. cm.
   Includes index.
   ISBN 0-13-061943-4
   1. Alien labor--United States--Handbooks, manuals, etc. 2. Job hunting--United States--Handbooks, manuals, etc. I. Williams, Anna Graf.

HD8081.A51535 2002
650.14'086'91-dc21   200207062

Editor-in-Chief: Stephen Helba
Executive Editor: Vernon R. Anthony
Executive Assistant: Nancy Kesterson
Editorial Assistant: Ann Brunner
Director of Manufacturing and Production: Bruce Johnson
Managing Editor: Mary Carnis
Developmental Editor: David E. Morrow
Manufactoring Buyer: Cathleen Peterson
Senior Production Editor: Adele M. Kupchik
Design Coordinator: Christopher Weigand
Interior Design & Formatting: Learnovation, LLC
Marketing Manager: Ryan DeGrote
Marketing Assistant: Eliabeth Farrell
Senior Marketing Coordinator: Adam Kloza
Electronic Art Creation: Karen J. Hall
Copy Editor: H. Muriel Adams
Proofreader: Cheryl Pontius
Text & Cover Printer/Binder: Phoenix Book Tech
Cover Designer: Kevin Kall

Prentice-Hall International (UK) Limited, *London*
Prentice-Hall of Australia Pty. Limited, *Sydney*
Prentice-Hall Canada Inc., *Toronto*
Prentice-Hall Hispanoamericana, S.A., *Mexico*
Prentice-Hall of India Private Limited, *New Delhi*
Prentice-Hall of Japan, Inc., *Tokyo*
Prentice-Hall Singapore Pte. Ltd.
Editora Prentice-Hall do Brasil, Ltda., *Rio de Janeiro*

Copyright © 2003 by Pearson Education, Inc., Upper Saddle River, New Jersey 07458. All rights reserved. Printed in the United States of America. This publication is protected by Copyright and permission should be obtained from the publisher prior to any prohibited reproduction, storage in a retrieval system, or transmission in any form or by any means, electronic, mechanical, photocopying, recording, or likewise. For information regarding permission(s), write to: Rights and Permissions Department.

10 9 8 7 6 5 4 3 2 1
ISBN 0-13-061943-4

Contents

Chapter 1 Only in America   1

America—Melting Pot or Fruit Salad? 2

Learning "American" Ways 3

The Freedom of America 3
    Religion 3
    Lifestyle 4
    Infrastructure 4
    Employment 4
    Government 5

Why America? 6
    Hopes and Dreams 6

Jobs, Skills, and the American Workplace 6
    Work Ethics 6
    On the Job 6
    Look at Your Skills 7

Overcoming Culture 7
    The War on Terrorism Is Not a War on Immigrants 7

Rules for Success 8

Summary 10

Glossary 10

Exercises 10

Chapter 2 Here to Stay! Immigration and Citizenship   13

INS—The Immigration and Naturalization Services 13

Types of Immigrants 14
    Permanent Residents (Green Card Holders) 14
    Non-Immigrants 15
    Asylees and Refugees 16
    Undocumented Immigrants—Illegal Aliens 17
    Parolees 17

Applying to Be a Permanent Resident 17
Family-Based Visa 17
Employment-Based Visa 18
Getting an Immigrant Visa Number 18
Health Issues That Might Keep You Out of the United States 19

Becoming a U.S. Citizen—Naturalization 20
The Naturalization Process 21
Losing Your Citizenship 22

Other Documents Needed to Work in the United States 22
Social Security Card 22
I-9 Forms 23

Summary 24

Resources for Immigration and Naturalization 24
Books 24
Websites 24

Glossary 25

Exercises 26

CHAPTER 3 LEARNING THE LANGUAGE   27

Learning the Language 27
Go to a Class 29
On the Job 29
Teach Yourself 29

Understanding the American Language 30
American English Is Different 30
Speaking the Language 32
Listening 32

Nonverbal Communication 33
Gestures 33
Body Movement and Posture 34
Space 34
Facial Expressions and Eye Contact 35
Using Your Voice 35
Clothing 35

Touch 35

Summary 36

Resources 36
    Website 36

Glossary 36

Exercises 36

CHAPTER 4 HYGIENE, GROOMING, AND CLOTHING   39

Sanitation and Hygiene 40
    Toilet Facilities 40
    Washing Your Hands 41
    Drying Your Hands 42
    Physically Disabled Access 43
    Baby-Changing Stations 43
    Feminine Hygiene 43
    Safer Sex 44

Hygiene—Keeping Clean 45
    Bathing/Showering 45
    Perfume and Cologne 46

Grooming—How You Look 48
    Hair 48
    Jewelry 48
    Body Piercing 50
    Tattoos 50

Clothing 50
    Dressing for the Job 50
      54
    Shoes 54

Personal Services 54

Summary 55

Glossary 55

Exercises 57

Chapter 5 Cash and Credit   59

Cash/Currency 59

Banks and Bank Accounts 60
- Bank Services 60
- Checking Accounts 61
- Savings Accounts 62
- Certificate of Deposits and Investments 62
- Loans and Mortgages 62
- Retirement Accounts 63
- Depositing Money in an Account 64

Credit Cards 64
- Your Credit Rating 65
- Types of Credit Cards 65
- Monthly and Revolving Charge Accounts 65
- Gold, Platinum, and Standard Cards 66
- Secure Credit Cards 66
- Managing Your Credit Cards 66

Summary 67

Resources 67

Glossary 68

Exercises 70

Chapter 6 Housing   71

Common Housing Options in the United States 71

Renting 72
- Things to Look for When Renting 73
- Renter's Insurance 74

Buying a House 74
- Know What You Want 75
- Finding aHouse to Buy 75
- Selecting a House 76
- The Mortgage 77
- Closing Costs 77

Contents

    Homeowner's Insurance and Taxes 78

Getting Settled in Your New Home 78
    Utilities 79
    Telephone 79
    Other Services 79
    Appliances 80
    Getting Your Mail 81

Moving In 82

Summary 82

Glossary 82

Exercises 84

CHAPTER 7 TRANSPORTATION   85

Getting Around in the United States 85

Local Transportation 85
    Buses 85
    Commuter Trains and the Subway 86
    Taxi Service 87

Driving a Car in the United States 88
    Getting a Driver's License 88

Owning a Car 90
    Buying a Car 91
    Financing the Car 91
    Automobile Insurance 92
    License Plates 93
    Emissions Testing 93
    Caring for Your Car 93

Driving on the Road 94
    Lanes and Exits 95

Summary 95

Glossary 96

Exercises 97

CHAPTER 8 SHOPPING   99

So Many Choices... 99

Where to Shop 99
    Supermarkets/Grocery Stores 99
    Department Stores 100
    Superstores 100
    Discount Stores 101
    Convenience Stores 101
    Drugstore/Pharmacy 102
    Wholesale Clubs 102
    Specialty Stores 102
    Shopping Mall 103
    Strip Mall 104
    Outlet Malls/Factory Outlets 104
    Farmer's Market 104
    Garage Sale/Yard Sale 105
    Flea Market 105

Shopping Basics 106
    Understand the Value of Your Money 106
    Where You Shop Will Affect the Price You Pay 106
    Pay the Price Listed—Do Not Barter 106
    Sales Tax 107
    Comparison Shopping 107
    Brand-Name Products 107
    Sales 108
    Bar Coding and Pricing 108
    Coupons 108
    Save Your Receipts 108
    Tipping for Services 109
    Catalogs 109

Shopping for Clothes 110

Clothing Size Chart 111
    Women's Clothing 111

Men's Clothing 112
Shirts 112
Shoes 112
Children's Clothing 113

Summary 113

Glossary 113

Exercises 116

CHAPTER 9 DINING IN, DINING OUT — 117

Grocery Shopping 117
Ethnic Groceries 117
Health Food Stores 118
Meat, Poultry, and Fish 118
Fruits and Vegetables 119
Prepackaged Foods 119

Dining Out—Eating Out 120
Types of Restaurants 120
The American Restaurant Experience 122
Tipping 123

Eating with Other People 123
Good Manners Are Important 124
Eating Family Style 124

Summary 125

Glossary 125

Exercise 126

CHAPTER 10 OUT ON YOUR OWN — 127

Agreements with Your Mentor 127
Am I a Guest or Family? 127
How Long to Stay? 128

Mixing and Mingling 130

Making Your Own Decisions 130
Setting Goals—Making It Happen 130

Getting a Plan—How You Will Achieve Your Goals 131
Getting What You Need 132

Moving Out on Your Own 132
Affording It All 132

Summary 133

Glossary 133

Exercises 134

CHAPTER 11 BALANCING HOME AND WORK   135

Taking Care of Your Family 135
Childcare 136
Day Care 136
Preschool 137
After School Programs 137
Care of the Elderly 137
When Someone Is Sick 138

Medical Care In America 138
The Doctor's Office 138
Clinics and Walk-in Medical Center 139
The Hospital/Emergency Room 140
Surgery and Outpatient Surgery 140
Pre-Approval 140
Co-pay 141
Prescription Drugs 141
Dentist and Dental Care 141
Eye Care 142
Immunizations and Preventative Drugs 142
Over-the-Counter Drugs 143
Natural Remedies 143

Safety and Security 144
Keeping Yourself and Your Family Safe 144
Defending Yourself 144
When You Have an Emergency 145

Understanding Time in America 146

Holidays and Traditions 146
American Holidays 146
Other Holidays 148
Religious Holidays 149
Special Events 149

Vacationing in the United States 151
Air Travel 151
Train Travel 152
Bus Travel 152
Car Travel 152
Road Safety 152
Laws of the Road 153
Lodging 153
Camping 153
The Convention and Visitors' Bureau 154
Local Library and Bookstores 154
Eating Out 154
Travel with Identification 154

Summary 155

Glossary 155

Exercises 157

CHAPTER 12 EDUCATION   159

Expanding Your Education 159
Transferring Your Education from Home 160
Professional Certifications 160
Individual Classes 160
Seminars and Workshops 161

The American Education System 161
Public vs. Private Schools 161
Grades and Grade Levels 162

Advanced Education 164
Bachelor's Degree 164
Associate Degree 165
Technical Colleges 165

Summary 165

Glossary 166

Exercises 166

CHAPTER 13 GETTING A JOB AND KEEPING A JOB   169

Before You Start Looking for a Job 169

Finding Job Openings 170
   Network with Your Friends 170
   Newspapers 170
   Help Wanted Signs 170
   Walk In and Ask 171
   Local Radio Stations, Cable TV, and Fliers 171
   The Internet 171
   Hiring Agencies 171

Preparing for the Job Application Process 172
   Documentation 172
   References 172
   Work Samples 172

Getting Ready for the Interview 173
   Questions 173

Filling Out a Job Application 173

Resumés 174

Interviewing for a Job 175
   Starting the Interview 175
   During the Interview 175
   Ending the Interview 175

Wages/Benefits 175
   Salary vs. Hourly—What Is the Difference? 176
   Pay Periods 176
   Work Hours 176
   Benefits 176

You Got the Job; Workplace Guidelines 177
   How to Act on Your First Day 177
   Hints on Time! 177

    Calling In or Not Coming to Work 178
    Attitude 178
    Training 178
    Company Culture 179
    Understanding Diversity in the American Workplace 179
    Company Policies 180
    Smoking 181

Summary 181

Glossary 181

Exercises 182

CHAPTER 14 TAXES AND ON-THE-JOB BENEFITS 185

Taxes 186
    Types of Taxes 186

How Do Benefits Work? 187
    When Do You Pay for Benefits? 187
    Pretax Option 188

Health Benefits 188
    Life Insurance 188
    Health Insurance 188
    Vision Coverage 189
    Dental Coverage 189
    Elective Insurance 190

Savings and Investment Benefits 190
    401(K) Savings Plans 190
    Pension Plans 191
    Stock Options 191

Additional Benefits 191
    Sick Days 191
    Vacation Days 191
    Holidays 191
    Paid Time Off 192
    Funeral (Bereavement) Leave 192
    Leaves of Absence 192
    Long-Term Leave of Absence 192

Family Medical Leave Act 193

Summary 193

Glossary 193

Exercises 195

CHAPTER 15 COMMUNICATION AT WORK   197

Learn to Listen 197
    Ways to Check if You Understood 197

Speaking Clearly 198

Use Questions to Manage Workplace Communication 198

Learning What to Write 199

Talking to the Boss 200

Talking to Your Co-Workers 200

Resolving Conflict 201

Talking to the Customer 203

Electronic Communication 203
    E-Mail 203
    Language on E-Mail 203

Summary 204

Glossary 204

Exercises 205

CHAPTER 16 TELEPHONES AND OTHER TECHNOLOGY   207

Telephones 207
    Your Local Phone Company 207
    Phone Basics 208
    Long-Distance Phone Service 209
    Billing 209
    International Calling 210
    Phone Cards 210
    Dial 10-10-xxx 210
    900 numbers 211

Directory Assistance 211
Telephone Solicitation 211
Pay Phones 212
Cellular Phones 212

Pagers 213

Fax Machines 214

Technology in the Workplace 214
Answering the Telephone 214
Cell Phones and Pagers 215

Summary 215

Glossary 215

Exercises 216

CHAPTER 17 MASS COMMUNICATION   219

Television (TV) 219
Television Access 220
Network Programming 220
Cable TV 221

Types of Television Programs 222
News Programs 222
Talk Shows 223
Game Shows 223

Radio 223

Newspapers and Magazines 224

The Internet 225
Internet Browsers and Search Engines 226

Summary 227

Glossary 227

Exercises 228

CHAPTER 18 FINDING AND BEING A MENTOR   229

Mentors Are There to Help You 229

Rules for the Mentor/Immigrant Relationship 230
    Mentor and Immigrant 230
    For the Mentor 230
    Having a Family Member as a Mentor 231
    Small Groups and Organizations 231

Mentoring Activities 232

Summary 234

Glossary 234

Exercise 234

GLOSSARY   237

APPENDIX A   VOCABULARY TO KNOW   253

APPENDIX B   STUDENT VISAS ARE NOT ALL THE SAME!   255

INDEX   257

Dedication

To all of our immigrant ancestors who had the courage to face a new world and search for a better life for their families, and in turn, for us.

Acknowledgements

Many people worked behind the scenes to help make this book happen. We would like to thank David Morrow and George Williams for all their time and effort on researching information, laying out the book, and proofing more than they ever wanted; Cheryl Pontius for her editing efforts; Rob Croese and his team of translators who gave us a first read through the book and suggested ways to make the text easier to read for immigrants; and finally to those many immigrants who gave us their time and excellent insights into America.

Preface

If you are reading this book, you are probably one of the following:

- a new immigrant to the United States
- someone who is planning on visiting the United States
- an exchange student from outside the United States
- a person who has a friend or relative who is coming to work or live in the United States
- a manager or mentor of a new immigrant.

Getting Ahead

This book was written to give immigrants an easy-to-read, direct look at daily life in the United States and the American workplace. People have always come to the United States to find new opportunities and to make a better life for themselves and their families. America offers many jobs and many choices, both personally and professionally.

Use this book to build your confidence and get ahead faster in the workplace. Learn what to expect at home and on the job. The more you know about America, the easier it will be to understand and work with your co-workers and managers on the job.

Getting Started

America is always changing and growing. People bring the best of their traditions and culture from all over the world, making America a blend of many different countries. Leaving behind friends and family and starting in a new country is not easy. Learning to understand and communicate with new people can be challenging.

This book provides basic information about the language, people, culture, and workplaces of America. We have used easy-to-read sentence structure and grammar to make it easier for people who are just learning English.

The Immigrant's Guide to the American Workplace: Making It in America is designed to cover essential information on many topics. We do not go too deeply into each topic, but give you enough information to understand America and to be successful in the workplace. You will find information on:

- learning the language
- communicating in the workplace

- hygiene and dress expectations
- how to use transportation
- shopping
- eating and dining
- managing money
- education for adults and children
- managing your health
- security and safety
- getting a job.

Using This Book

You will find several features in the book to help you learn about the United States. Look for feature boxes in each chapter containing important information. Complete the exercises at the end of each chapter to learn even more about the topics discussed. Improve your vocabulary by working through the extra exercises in Appendix A.

> **IN THIS CHAPTER**
> - American shopping
> - Types of stores America has to offer
> - Where to get what you need
> - How to shop in America
> - Clothes shopping

In this Chapter:

The information discussed in the chapter.

 *A Word from Kooner...* Look for mentor and immigrant experiences from author Daljinder Kooner.

Immigrant Views

Watch for immigrant advice under "Immigrant Views."

About the Authors

Each of the authors brought his/her own unique skills, ethnic backgrounds and experiences to the development of this book:

Anna Graf Williams, Ph.D., is a second-generation, born-in-America German who went from being a farmer's daughter to earning a Ph.D. in education. As the co-founder and co-owner of Learnovation®, LLC, she has designed and taught courses in diversity, mentored immigrant students in the hotel and restaurant business, and worked with people to expand their careers.

Daljinder Kooner brought the initial inspiration and insight into the writing team as a naturalized citizen – 20 years in the United States – from India. He has helped mentor and introduce many of his family and friends to the United States, and is a successful entrepreneur and restaurateur.

Mary Jo Dolasinski is Croatian, second-generation, born in America. She is a corporate trainer in the lodging and restaurant industry – one of the biggest employers of immigrant workers in the United States. Mary Jo has many years of management experience with a multi-ethnic work force. She also taught ethnic dance for 16 years and is a university instructor.

Karen J. Hall is one of those Americans with a mixed heritage. She has traces of English, Dutch, Scottish, and German ancestry and probably more thrown in for good measure—some who immigrated as early as the late 1600s and some in the 1870s. She has been a corporate trainer in the field of software doing instructional design and editing, a university instructor, and currently works with career development as a co-founder and co-owner of Learnovation®, LLC.

One of our challenges in putting together a book like this is presenting information for a wide group of diverse people from all over the world. People come with different expectations, different customs, and it is easy to take offense. What may be new information to one person may be a way of life to another. Please take from this book what you need and apply it to your own life. Use this book to build your confidence and get ahead faster in the workplace. Learn what to expect at home and on the job.

We are glad you are here – Welcome to the American workplace!

Chapter 1

Only in America

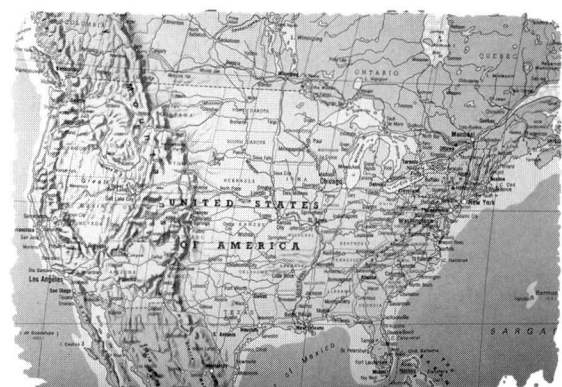

In America, you can succeed by working hard. Only in America ... can you become an American. Welcome to the United States of America! In America, there will be new experiences and the chance to preserve your own traditions. You have choices. Choices are what make the United States of America!

Your choices are many, ranging from where you live, to what you wear, where you work, what you eat, and what you make of yourself. In each part of your life, you will be flooded with decisions to make.

As we wrote this book, we realized we had to talk about American culture, ideas, and the practical day-to-day activities of living in the United States in addition to the American workplace. The American worker is a total person, who has to be personally successful. And, being successful in the workplace will help you be successful in the United States.

Why do immigrants choose the United States of America? Some say it is to have:

- A better life
- The opportunity to work
- The freedom to choose
- The freedom to speak freely
- The chance to practice any religion
- The chance to be in a free country.

This book will take an honest look at the American workplace—the hopes, the dreams, the opportunities and many of the challenges. True to the ideals which this country was built upon, this book deals with

> **In This Chapter**
>
> - A nation of immigrants
> - Freedoms America offers
> - Job skills in the American workplace
> - Overcoming culture
> - Getting started: rules for success

the whole person. You will be given a chance to explore everything from finding a mentor to getting a job. This book is filled with basics and good practices.

In this book, we have used the term **immigrant** for anyone who is coming to live and work in the United States from another country and culture – whether short-term, migrant worker, or permanent resident.

America—Melting Pot or Fruit Salad?

You will discover as soon as you arrive that America is made up of many kinds of people. We do not look, act, or believe in the same way. In the past, immigrants who came to America wanted to adapt to the American way of life as quickly and completely as possible. Many immigrants discarded their traditions and ways of life to blend with the current American culture. America was called a "melting pot." Each person who came to the country blended in.

The American Melting Pot

Today, people approach adaptation to the United States differently. People now bring their traditions, cultures, values, and tastes with them and try to preserve them. You do not have to abandon your native culture to become an American. You could think of America as a fruit salad. Each part of the salad is separate, but united. When you bite a grape, you will taste the grape, but you will also taste the sauce. Qualities of America cover each of us, but we are still always individuals.

American Fruit Salad

In writing this book, we have had to make some generalized statements about Americans. It is very difficult to generalize about Americans. No matter what we write, someone will disagree with a piece of it, or be offended by it. This is something great about America; people can voice their opinions. Voicing your opinion means to say what you think. In America this is OK (OK = acceptable).

This book is designed to be a general guide to the U.S. culture and workplace. Your experiences may be very different depending on where you live and what you do. This book is written at a basic level so it can be read by people who may still be learning English. Everyone comes to America with different experiences and background. Consider this book as a place to start.

Learning "American" Ways

It would be easier for us to help you if we had a list of specific "American" ways, but ways constantly change. A few significant things to know about the United States are:

- Anyone qualified for a job may apply for the job to receive equal pay
- Timeliness is important and being on time is expected
- Men and women are considered equal
- There are laws to protect children from abuse, including child labor laws
- Cleanliness, safety, and sanitation are valued and expected
- Anyone may speak about any beliefs or ideas
- Anyone may ask any question without fear of punishment
- You can competitively shop for goods and services
- You can choose your medical care
- Anyone in the United States may travel to anywhere else in the United States without permission
- Everyone has the right to succeed or fail on individual merits
- Technology is valued
- Laws are viewed with respect.

The Freedom of America

Religion

An important freedom in America is religion. You may practice any religion you choose. You may worship in the faith of your choosing, with the beliefs you choose, and you may discuss your religion in public.

Lifestyle

"Life, liberty, and the pursuit of happiness" are key beliefs in the United States. You may live where you want. You may live with whom you wish. You can eat what you wish, seek medical attention as you choose, and purchase goods you can pay for in the marketplace. You may get your driver's license and drive anywhere in the country. You may put your money in any bank. You may use the telephones and computers as you are able.

America has an economy based upon capitalism. You may secure almost any goods and services you can pay for.

Infrastructure

Our communities consist of many building blocks. Government at the national, state, and local levels are all part of the **infrastructure**. The infrastructure is all the underlying features of the political and social systems that serve the people of an area.

Computers, telephones, roads, sewers, electrical power, water, police, fire, and emergency rescue are a few of the pieces of our infrastructure. These services are all part of our communities.

"From what I accomplished in my lifetime, here so far with my family, I strongly believe and understand the truth about the saying 'America is the land of opportunity.'"

Peter Eder is 100 years old and has lived in this country 65-plus years.

Employment

Now that you are in the United States, you have the American workplace to help you earn what you want. The ability to work in any chosen field where you have the skills, knowledge, and desire is an important part of America. You can seek out a job, apply, participate in interviews, and get a job. With the proper training, you can have any career you wish.

Government

The United States is made up of 50 separate states. The states vary in size and organization, but each state has its own government, leadership, courts, and sets of laws. People in the United States can travel and move from one state to another without any restrictions or papers.

The United States is a **republic**—meaning the people elect representatives to make the laws. Each state is divided into counties or parishes, with each county/parish having laws and courts. Each city or town in the county/parish also has its own leadership with laws and services.

We also have a national system of government. The people in each state elect officials to represent their ideas in the national government. The national, or federal, government includes the president of the United States, the Congress, and the federal courts. The federal government provides services to the states. It also provides protection to citizens and represents America to other countries.

The goal of the government is to help all Americans be safe, peaceful, and prosperous. The Constitution is the basis for all American laws. Federal laws may have priority over state laws. State laws take priority over the local laws. A key issue that makes the United States of America different than many other countries is a separation of personal, religious, and political matters. This is referred to as the "separation of church and state." This means the government does not decide where or how you choose to worship. Separating personal and public matters is very important to people in the United States.

There are several things the government does not do. The government does not pay for most health care. The government also does not own banks or churches. The government does have laws that monitor and regulate banks and hospitals. These laws are intended to protect people from dangerous or dishonest practices.

Why America?

Some people come to this country to escape hardship. Others come to make their fortune. And still others may come to join family.

Throughout its history, the United States of America has been a destination for immigrants. A desire for hard work and freedom of choice are what we all share in common.

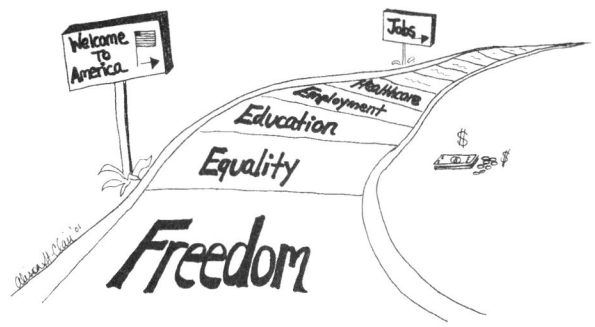

People come to America for many reasons.

Hopes and Dreams

Many people have hopes and dreams of something better. In America, you can set a goal, choose a way to reach it, and go after it. Almost anything you can visualize can happen.

A search for a better life is what America has been built upon. Your own philosophy can power your success. If you believe you can do something, you can do it.

Jobs, Skills, and the American Workplace

The United States of America now has one of the lowest unemployment rates in an open economy country. America has moved from an agricultural society to an industrial society, and now to a society based on information. People in the workforce do many different things. Some people work in a factory. Other people work as financial managers. Other people work in kitchens and restaurants. There are many different kinds of jobs you can have. As you get ready to look for a job, there are several things you can do to make finding a job easier.

Work Ethics

People in the American workplace can have very different work ethics. A person's **work ethic** is a set of values based on the belief in hard work and effort. Some people think their work is most important. Other people think their family is more important than work. Everyone may have a different idea of what "hard work" is.

On the Job

In the American workforce, women may work next to men; people of different races, and different religious values may work together. Your family background, your gender, and your ownership of land do not impact your ability to earn money, achieve in business, or your position in a company. Employers in America may also seem very different. While employers may have government regulations and some employment laws, the desire to make money drives decision making. Here are things to think about when you looking for a job:

- ✦ Know what type of job you want
- ✦ Understand what benefits are available
- ✦ Plan for your future.

You can have more than just a job; you can have a career. A career is a lifelong path of dedication to a type of profession or industry. Careers are based on skills, training, and your chosen profession.

Look at Your Skills

You may have education or training you received in your home country. Identify how you can use your skills and training in the American workplace. There are several ways to do this. Your education from your home country may be accepted in the United States. If your education is not directly recognized by your chosen industry, explore how you can apply your knowledge to gain certifications and to fulfill educational requirements. There are many groups that help guide professionals. Contact them for more specific information. If you have access to a computer, investigate options on the Internet.

Overcoming Culture

Many people who come to America are self-conscious. Relax. While we all share in our commitment to freedom, we are each very different. Meet and be friends with people who are not like you. In this book, ***The Immigrant's Guide to the American Workplace***, we will spend time discussing ways to succeed in the American work force.

The War on Terrorism Is Not a War on Immigrants

On September 11, 2001, four commercial planes were hijacked by terrorists and used as weapons to destroy the World Trade Center in New York and to damage the Pentagon in Washington, D.C., killing thousands of U. S. citizens and immigrants alike. Because of the terrorist attacks on the United States, the United States has increased restrictions on immigration. The hijackers were born outside the United States. Many of them came to this country on visas. The President and Congress declared a war on terrorism, which means we have government agencies inside and troops outside the country working to bring these hijackers and their associates to justice.

This day in history was emotional, concerning, and challenging for many Americans, some of whom responded by racial profiling. **Racial profiling** is the use of distinctive features or characteristics, such as race, by which pre-judgments are made. Many immigrants with racial profiles similar to the hijackers found themselves being challenged in everything from service to being questioned about their activities and employment.

At the writing of this book, immigration laws are under review. The government immigrant record-keeping practices are also under revision. For example, immigrants on student visas will now have additional registration appointments to keep at universities. You may have to answer more questions, experience longer waiting times as these issues are worked out. Please be patient. We believe it is worth it to be in the United States of America.

Rules for Success

If immigrants asked us this question: **"If you could give one piece of advice to new immigrants, to make their life easier, What would it be?"**

- **Learn English.** You will have more opportunities and an easier transition.
- **Do not be afraid to speak the language.** Many immigrants told us they understand what is being said but are afraid to speak English. They do not want to make mistakes. Making mistakes is a natural part of learning a language. You will learn more quickly by trying to speak.
- **Have a clean body.** Americans are sensitive to body odors. People in the United States are offended by strong body odors.
- **Learn how to communicate with other people.** Do not be afraid to meet people, even if those people are different from you.
- **Find a mentor.** Find a person from your family or a friend to help you. If you do not have family in the United States, try to meet other people to find a mentor.
- **Work for what you want.**
- **Have a positive attitude.** You can do anything you decide to do. Make goals and work toward them.
- **Be prepared for differences.** America may be very different from your home country. You will find things you like and things you do not like in America.
- **Not everyone in the United States is like what you may have seen on television.**
- **Relax, enjoy, and be open to new opportunities.** This book will help you become familiar with how to be successful in America.

Summary

The United States of America is a land of immigrants. The American dream is one filled with the promise of a good life. There are many freedoms to be experienced from the freedom of speech to the right to own property. The United States is rich with culture. You may need to overcome some culture shock along your road to success. Now that you have an overview, we will take a look at what to expect when you live and work in the United States.

Glossary

County: local government.

Discrimination: people judging others based on their appearance.

Immigrant: in this book, anyone who is coming to live and work in the United States from another country and culture – whether short-term, migrant worker, or permanent resident.

Infrastructure: the underlying features of the political and social systems that serve the people of an area.

Racial profiling: the use of distinctive features or characteristics such as race by which prejudgments are made.

Republic: the people elect representatives to make the laws.

Work ethic: a person's set of values based on the belief in hard work and effort.

Exercises

1. Internet Exercise (see Pages 213-214 for more information on the Internet): Log on to any search engine (www.google.com, www.dogpile.com, www.yahoo.com) and search by the following terms to learn more about immigration in America:
   - Immigrant
   - United States, Map
   - U.S. Constitution
   - Immigrant stories.

2. Interview two people and ask them "What does it mean to you to live in America?" One person should be born in America and one should be an immigrant. Make a list of what is important to each. How are their perceptions the same or different?

CHAPTER 2

HERE TO STAY! IMMIGRATION AND CITIZENSHIP

Each year, the United States issues more than 31.4 million visas to visitors, workers, and people who want to live and work in the United States. You can get a visa for a short stay, or you can apply for permanent residency. How do you get a visa to live in the United States? How can you become a citizen? This chapter deals with some of the issues of immigrating to America. **Note:** The information in this book should NOT be used to replace legal advice for immigration issues.

This chapter is for anyone who:

✦ Is in the United States and wants to stay here

✦ Is abroad and wants to know how to legally enter the United States

✦ Wants to become a citizen of the United States of America

✦ Employs, teaches, or is a friend or family member of someone dealing with immigration or citizenship issues.

INS—The Immigration and Naturalization Services

The **INS,** or (**Immigration and Naturalization Services**), is the currently a part of the U.S. government that controls the immigration process. The United States government is reviewing the INS for possible changes. We encourage you to read this chapter to help you understand immigration terms and to use

IN THIS CHAPTER

- About the INS (Immigration and Naturalization Services)
- Types of immigrants
- Types of visas
- How to become a resident of the United States
- How to get a visa number
- How to become a U.S. citizen
- Other documents needed to work in the United States

the resources listed on page 22 to find the most updated information on immigration procedures.

Types of Immigrants

U.S. immigration law divides all people into two groups, U.S. citizens and aliens. A **U.S. citizen** is any person who was born in the United States or who has been naturalized (granted full citizenship), unless they have given up their rights to citizenship in America. The term **alien** refers to people who are not U.S. citizens. Immigrants seeking to work in the United States fall into the following categories:

- Permanent residents (green card holders)
- Non-immigrants
- Asylees
- Refugees
- Undocumented immigrants ("illegal aliens")
- Parolees.

All people, except undocumented immigrants who are in the country without approval by the INS, have the freedom to travel throughout the United States. However, they may experience limitations based upon the type of visa or status.

Permanent Residents (Green Card Holders)

Permanent residents are aliens who have permission to live and work in the United States. They pay taxes in the United States and can travel freely in and out of the country. Permanent residents are sometimes called green card holders, lawful permanent residents, or lawful immigrants. Permanent residents are given a **permanent resident card**, formerly called an alien registration card. This used to be known as a green card, because the first cards were green. Now the cards are pink and have a permanent plastic coating.

Travel Outside the United States—Permanent residents can travel freely in and out of the United States. However, if the permanent resident leaves the country for more than six

Welcome to America

months, the INS has the right to question if the card holder has given up residence. A re-entry permit should be secured before you leave the United States.

If you are out of the country more than two years, you must plan to reapply for a new re-entry permit. Some reasons people get re-entry permits are:

- To work temporarily outside the country
- To care for a relative who is sick
- To study abroad.

If you are out of the country for more than one year without a re-entry permit, you can get a returning resident visa. If you try to come back without a returning resident visa, you could be denied entry to the United States.

Maintaining Your Residence—If a permanent resident anticipates being out of the country more than six months, he or she must be prepared to prove he or she is still paying taxes, has a bank account, and a permanent residence. You must also explain why you were out of the country. If you are out of the United States for more than one year, your green card cannot be used for re-entry.

Non-Immigrants

Non-immigrants are short-stay, non-resident, non-citizens who are working in the United States with the intention of returning to their home. Non-immigrants require a temporary, or non-immigrant, visa. Procedures and rules for non-immigrant entry are designed to assist temporary entry of foreign persons for employment, and still protect border security, local labor, and permanent employment.

Business Travel—The following non-immigrant visa categories are available to aliens who will be in the United States for a short time:

- **B-1 Visas**: Business visitors
- **E-1 and E-2 Visas**: Treaty traders and investors
- **H-1 Visas:** Professionals in specialized occupations
- **J-1 Visas**: Exchange trainees
- **TN Visas**: Canadian and Mexican professionals and consultants
- **L-1 Visas**: Intra-company transferees
- **O Visas**: Aliens with extraordinary ability
- **P Visas**: Performing artists and athletes

+ **R Visas**: Religious workers.

Eligibility—To receive any type of non-immigrant visa you must demonstrate that:

+ Your stay is temporary.
+ You have sufficient funds to support yourself while visiting the United States (unless your visa status allows you to work).
+ You will retain your foreign national residence if you have a non-immigrant visa other than E-1, H-1, B-1, or L-1.

Types of Documentation—Documentation proves you have permanent ties to your country, such as a job to which you will return, a bank account, home ownership, or family ties. Types of documentation could include:

+ A letter from your company to show your stay is temporary
+ A bank statement showing sufficient funds
+ A copy of a deed or title showing proof of ownership of a residence.

Conditions and Restrictions—You agree to respect the limitations of your visa. The immigration officer determines:

+ If you are intending to immigrate
+ If you are excludable from the United States or
+ How long you will be allowed to stay in the United States (A completed I-94 departure form will be attached to your passport. The amount of time you are eligible to stay in the United States may not be the amount of time granted for your stay.)

Changing Your Status—Any foreign national who enters the United States under any type of non-immigrant classification can apply for another type of non-immigrant status.

Asylees and Refugees

Asylees, because of race, religion, nationality, political opinions, or memberships in a particular group, have come to the United States to avoid being persecuted in their home country. They apply to INS for asylum either after they enter or during entry to the United States. **Refugees** are also people who are afraid of persecution. Refugees are assigned refugee status before coming to the United States. Both asylees and refugees are eligible to adjust to lawful permanent resident status after one year of continuous presence in the United States.

Undocumented Immigrants—Illegal Aliens

Undocumented immigrants are more often referred to as illegal aliens—they do not have permission to live or work in the United States. These include:

- People who evade inspection by an INS officer
- People who entered the United States by using falsified documents
- Tourists who entered with a valid non-immigrant visa but overstayed the time allowed.

Parolees

Parolees is the term for aliens who have not yet been approved for entry into the United States. The INS will automatically grant this status without its having been requested. This status is often granted while the INS investigates an alien's admissibility.

Applying to Be a Permanent Resident

The United States issues between 700,000 to 900,000 permanent resident visas each year. Depending on a number of factors, it may take several years before you are issued a permanent resident visa. Most people who apply for residency either have family in the United States or want to work here permanently.

Family-Based Visa

People who want to become immigrants are divided into categories based on a preference system. The immediate relatives of U.S. citizens, which includes parents, spouses, and unmarried children under the age of 21, do not have to wait for an immigrant visa number to become available once the application filed for them is approved by the INS. **An immigrant visa number will be immediately available for immediate relatives of U.S. citizens**. The relatives in the following categories must wait for a visa to become available in this order:

1. Unmarried, adult sons and daughters of U.S. citizens that are age 21 or older.
2. Spouses of lawful permanent residents and unmarried sons and daughters, regardless of age.
3. Married sons and daughters of U.S. citizens and their spouses and children.
4. Brothers and sisters of adult U.S. citizens, their spouses and their children under the age of 21.

Employment-Based Visa

People who want to immigrate based on employment must wait for an immigration visa number to become available. The following preferences are followed in order:

1. Priority workers, including aliens with extraordinary abilities, outstanding professors and researchers, and certain multi-national executives and managers.
2. Members of professions holding advanced degrees or persons of exceptional ability.
3. Skilled workers, professionals, and other qualified workers.
4. Certain special immigrants, including those in religious vocations.
5. Employment creation immigrants.

If you must wait for a number, your application will be processed, and the number will be issued in the order your application was received.

Getting an Immigrant Visa Number

Here are the basic steps to getting a permanent resident visa:

- File an immigrant visa petition. These are usually filed by a relative or by an employer (the petitioner) for you (the beneficiary). You may need to personally fill out the application and pay any fees.
- A visa number is made available to you by the U.S. State Department.
    - The INS will tell the petitioner whether or not the visa petition is approved.
    - The INS will send the approved visa petition to the Department of State's National Visa Center. It will remain there until an immigration number is available. The Center will notify you (the beneficiary) when the visa petition is received. They will also notify the beneficiary when an immigrant visa number is available.
    You should contact the National Visa Center if you have a change of address. You can send mail to the Visa Center at: The National Visa Center; 32 Rochester Avenue; Portsmouth, New Hampshire 03801-2909; U.S.A.
    - How can you find out when an immigration visa number will be available? The date the petition was filed is known as your **priority date**. The U.S. State Department publishes a bulletin that shows the month and year of the visa petitions in progress by country and preference category. You may reference your priority date in the bulletin.

- If you are already in the United States when your immigration visa number becomes available:
  - You complete the process by being fingerprinted, having a medical exam from an approved INS physician, and showing proof of immunization.
  - If you are not in the United States, you can go to the local U.S. Consulate to complete processing.
    Note: If you are already in the United States, you may apply to adjust your permanent resident status.

United States law limits the number of immigrant visa numbers available every year. This means that even if the INS approves your immigrant visa petition you may not get an immigrant visa number immediately. In some cases, several years could pass between the time INS approves your immigrant visa petition, and the U.S. State Department gives you an immigrant visa number. In addition, U.S. law also limits the number of immigrant visas available by country. This means you may have to wait longer if you come from a country with a high demand for U.S. immigrant visas.

Health Issues That Might Keep You Out of the United States

You are ineligible for residence if you have the following medical conditions:

- Infectious tuberculosis
- AIDS or HIV
- Sexually transmitted diseases (STDs), such as syphilis and gonorrhea
- Mental retardation or mental illness.

If you are inadmissible because of a positive tuberculosis test or treatable diseases, you will be given time to obtain treatment and then may have a new medical examination.

Vaccinations—A **vaccination** is an injection of medication that helps the body protect itself from diseases. Immigration laws require immigrants provide proof of vaccination for the following diseases:

- Mumps
- Measles
- Rubella
- Polio

- Tetanus
- Diphtheria toxoids
- Pertussis
- Influenza type B
- Hepatitis B.

Depending on which country you are coming from, additional immunizations may be required.

Becoming a U.S. Citizen—Naturalization

Many immigrants want to become U.S. citizens. **Naturalization** is the process by which U.S. citizenship is granted to a permanent resident. As a citizen, you will be able to vote in elections and receive a U.S. passport. All U.S. citizens, whether born or naturalized, have the same rights, with one exception. Only a natural-born citizen may become president or vice president. Naturalized citizens may work in a federal job, vote, and hold public office.

You may apply to become a U.S. citizen if you:

- Have been a permanent resident for five years or more
- Have been married to and living with a U.S. citizen for three years while a permanent resident
- Are a child of a permanent resident, following the child citizenship procedures.

The Naturalization Process

You must apply for naturalization to the INS. Here is the basic process:

1. **Prepare for the Process** – Take classes in naturalization, English, civics (American Government).
2. **Complete the Application** – Submit an application for naturalization along with two photos and additional documents.
3. **Be Fingerprinted** – Receive an appointment letter from the INS to be fingerprinted. Get your fingerprints taken. Wait to receive an appointment for your interview.
4. **Interview and Test** – Go to the interview, bringing identification and any documents required. Answer questions about your application and background. Take the English and civics test. Receive a decision. If approved, you will receive a ceremony date to take your oath of allegiance.

5. **Ceremony to Take the Oath** – Check in at the ceremony, answer questions about what you have done since your interview, turn in your permanent resident card and take the oath of allegiance. You will receive a certificate of naturalization.

The Application—The United States requires you to accurately fill out a naturalization application. Being truthful is very important. You must:

- Give complete information on your name and address.
- Be able to speak, read, and write English. Some exceptions are made to the English requirement. Look for details in the laws about immigration.
- Be able to list and explain any and all absences from the United States.
- Have been physically present in the United States for at least half the time you have been a resident. Some exceptions are made for business travel, religious workers, people who work on the sea, people serving in the military, and people working for the U.S. government abroad.
- Give employment information.
- Give residence information.
- Give complete information on your marital history.
- Give information about any children you have.
- Answer questions about your character and beliefs.
- Give information on your mental health.
- Admit if you have committed a crime and/or have been arrested.
- List your present and past memberships in any clubs, groups, or organizations.

The Oath—During the allegiance oath, you will be asked to pledge allegiance to the United States by stating:

- Your belief in the Constitution
- An oath of allegiance to the United States
- Your willingness to bear arms for the United States
- Your willingness to perform non-combative services for the United States
- Your willingness to perform work of national importance under civilian direction.

Losing Your Citizenship

It is possible to lose your naturalized citizenship by:

- Committing fraud to get citizenship. If you lie about information on your application you may lose your citizenship.
- Committing an act of expatriation. An act of expatriation might be if you were to join a different government's political system.
- Renouncing your U.S. citizenship.

For any of these reasons, the INS can deport the former citizen.

Other Documents Needed to Work in the United States

Social Security Card

Once you have permission to work in the United States, you will need to set up a social security account. The government issues a number to every person in the United States. Your **social security number** is the number of your social security account and is used as a means of identification. Your social security number is uniquely yours. The number is used as proof of your identity and as a record-keeping tool.

You will need to use your social security number for several things including:

- Setting up bank accounts or credit accounts
- Signing insurance policies
- Attending school
- Proving your eligibility to work in the United States.

Go to the social security office in your city or community. You will need to take your visa and proof of your identity to apply for a social security number. Applying for a social security number should be one of the first things you do when arriving in the United States. You will need to establish a permanent address before going to a social security office.

Even children need a social security number. In the United States, parents apply for their child's social security number at birth. Once you have a social security card, you are not likely to need this office again until retirement. However, you will need to contact the social security office if you officially change your name (if you get married and want to use your spouse's last name).

As you work in the United States, taxes are taken out of your paycheck and are deposited with the government. Some of these taxes go into your social security fund. When you reach a certain age, or if you become disabled, you will be eligible to draw from this money on a monthly basis.

A Word from Kooner...

"Whenever I am mentoring a family member, the first place I take him or her is to the social security office. A social security number is needed to do almost everything from opening a bank account to filling out a job application. Then I show him/her the post office. We go in and talk through the change of address cards, show them the post office boxes, and the ways to ship packages overseas. Over the next couple of weeks, we discuss when to get a driver's license and what taxes are to be paid. I usually show him/her my pay stub and explain taxes."

I-9 Forms

Every person in the United States who works is required to complete an I-9 form before they can begin a job. The purpose of the I-9 is to verify your eligibility to work in the United States of America. You have three days from the date you are hired to complete the I-9 information for your employer. Not completing an I-9 can cause you to lose your job. If you have difficulty completing the form, ask a translator to help you. The translator will need to sign his or her name on the form.

Summary

Contact your local INS office to learn more about the immigration process or visit its website at www.ins.gov. It is very important to follow all the laws and procedures. It is also very important to maintain your legal status. If you do not understand something, ask someone for help. Keeping your documentation in order can make your new life in America successful!

Resources for Immigration and Naturalization

Books

Ivener, Mark A. *Handbook of Immigrant Law* (2000).

Wernick, Allan *U.S. Immigrant & Citizenship,* Revised. 2 ed., 1999.

Websites

http://www.insgreencard.com—A private company sharing advice and information on immigration.

http://www.ins.gov—A U.S. government site for Immigration and Naturalization

Keywords to Search By on the Internet

Immigration law

I-9 form

Naturalization

Social security number

Green card

Immunization

CDC, Centers for Disease Control

U.S. citizenship

Immigration visa

Temporary work visa

Glossary

Alien: people who are not citizens of the United States including permanent residents (green card holders), non-immigrants, asylees, refugees, parolees, and undocumented immigrants (illegal aliens).

Asylees: aliens who apply to INS for asylum, either after they enter or during entry to the United States, to avoid being persecuted in their home country.

Citizen: any person who was born in the United States or who has been naturalized (granted full citizenship), unless they have given up their rights to citizenship in America.

Immediate relatives of U.S. citizens: parents, spouses, and unmarried children under the age of 21.

Immigration and Naturalization Services (INS): the part of the United States government that controls the immigration process.

Naturalization: the process by which U.S. citizenship is granted to a permanent resident.

Parolees: aliens who, at the time they apply, are not admissible as non-immigrants or permanent residents.

Permanent resident card: a document issued to permanent residents. Formerly called an alien registration card. Sometimes known as a "green card."

Priority date: the date the immigrant visa petition was filed.

Refugees: aliens who apply for and are assigned refugee status before coming to the United States to avoid being persecuted in their home country.

Social security number: the number of your social security account, used as a means of identification by many organizations, schools, banks and the government.

Undocumented immigrants: more often referred to as illegal immigrants—they do not have permission to live or work in the United States.

Vaccination: an injection of medication that helps the body protect itself from diseases.

Exercises

1. Internet Exercise (see Pages 211-212 for more information on the Internet): Log onto any search engine (www.google.com, www.dogpile.com, www.yahoo.com) and search by the following terms to learn more about immigration and citizenship:

    - Immigration law
    - I-9 form
    - Naturalization
    - Social security number
    - "Green cards"
    - Immunization
    - CDC, Centers for Disease Control
    - U.S. citizenship
    - Immigration visa
    - Temporary work visa.

2. Develop your plan for getting your naturalized U.S. citizenship. Review the naturalization process in this chapter and set your own personal timelines and goals for becoming a U. S. citizen. Remember, to become a naturalized citizen you must:
    a. Have been a permanent resident for five or more years.
    b. Have been married, and living with, a U.S. citizen for three or more years.
    c. Be a child of a permanent resident.

    Your personal citizenship plan may take you a few months or five years depending on your eligibility and personal desire. Do not forget you have to be able to read, write, and speak English.

Chapter 3

Learning the Language

When coming to the United States, one of the most important things you can do is learn to speak English. We asked people who have immigrated to the United States to give advice to people just arriving here. In interview after interview, the answer was the same, "Learn the language." Learning English can make everything else easier! If you already know English, you may find American English to be very different. American English is always changing.

There is no official language in the United States, but most people speak English. All public signs and information are provided in English. As the immigrant population in the United States grows, more services are geared to people who do not speak English. There are many ethnic neighborhoods in cities where you will find signs, services, and radio stations in other languages. Spanish is often spoken in areas of the United States with large Hispanic populations, especially the South and Southwest. •any immigrants choose to live in an area where there are other people from their home country. It is much easier to adjust to the United States and begin to speak English when there are others to help you.

You also communicate in more than just words. Your body language, gestures, voice, expressions, and eye contact are very important. People tend to trust the body language more than a person's speech. The body language of Americans may be very different from what you are used to.

Learning the Language

When you speak English, it will be easier for you to get and keep a job. It can also help you to:

+ Find a job where you can make more money
+ •ake new friends

In This Chapter
▪ Ways to learn English
▪ Understanding American English - slang and jargon
▪ Nonverbal communication - body language and gestures
▪ Touch and physical space

- Keep learning new things
- Make America your home more quickly.

Go to a Class

Taking a class in English is a good way to learn to speak, write, and read. Many classes are geared to learning the basic words you will need to begin speaking in English. Classes are offered at many local high schools and universities. Communities with large immigrant groups may also offer classes. Most classes can teach you English well enough to help you get and keep a job. To learn more about classes, call a school near you and/or ask a friend for suggestions.

On the Job

If you already have a job, ask your boss about classes. Many companies offer **ESL (English as a Second Language)** classes to employees. These classes are usually free or may only cost a small amount. Some companies even allow members of your family to attend the classes. They are usually offered in the evenings or during your off hours.

Teach Yourself

There are also several ways to teach English to yourself. If classes are not available, or you cannot attend them, go to the local bookstore or public library. Most communities have a public library where you can go to borrow books, tapes, and videos that can teach you English. Ask your mentor for help obtaining a library card.

Learning the Language

The single most important skill to help you in the American workplace is the ability to speak English. There are several ways to improve your English:

- **Buy a dictionary** – look up the words you do not know.
- **Listen to the radio** – the more you hear the language, the more familiar it will be.
- **Look at the newspaper** – words will begin to make sense with the pictures. Start by reading the headlines first.
- **Read magazines on a regular basis** – they will help you learn about people and places.
- **Watch TV** – watch the news and listen to commercials, watch game shows and other programs.
- **Speak only in English** – even when your mentor or friends speak your home language. It is important to use the language so you learn it. Try to speak English on the job even if you are not perfect.
- **Use the Internet** – there are many sites that can give you practice learning English.

Books and Audiotapes—Books are great tools. However, it is difficult to learn a language by only using books. Hearing how words are said is very important when learning a language. Using audiotapes can help you hear words. Many tapes have a book to read as you listen to the tape.

Computer Programs and the Internet—If you have access to a computer, there are programs you can buy or rent to teach you English. Most of the computer learning programs have sound. The Internet has many websites for non native English speakers, or ESL speakers. The website ESL-Lab (www.esl-lab.com) includes listening and understanding exercises. These exercises let you listen to recorded conversations. You can quiz yourself on what has been said.

There are many ways to learn English.

Understanding the American Language

You may already know English but want to improve. There are several things you can do to improve your knowledge of the language. Watching television is helpful. Watching the news, talk shows, and educational shows can add to your **vocabulary,** or the number of words you know. Try to read the newspaper, magazines, etc. If you have access to a computer, use the Internet. It is a great way to read about a lot of different topics.

Use a dictionary to look up words you do not know.

American English Is Different

Many immigrants learn English before coming to the United States. They are often surprised when they do not understand what is being said. American English is very different from British English. Americans use some different words and tend to speak casually. Many training programs outside of the United States teach the language more formally than Americans speak it. An example of informal use of the language may be using the term "Guys and Gals" in place of the term "Ladies and Gentlemen."

Immigrant Views

"To learn the language in your own country and then come and live in America is totally different. Because there are a lot of phrases people will say to me and I have no clue what they mean."

Khulood Ankrom is a naturalized citizen working in the hotel industry.

Slang

American English is always changing. New words come into use, and others fall away. **Slang** is a casual word or expression. Some slang words may not be listed in the dictionary. Sometimes the words in a slang phrase mean something completely different from the individual words listed in the dictionary. Words can also mean opposite things depending on the tone of voice used. If you hear slang you do not understand, ask for an explanation of the word or phrase. Here is some common slang used in everyday language:

Common Slang Terms

Slang Term	What It Means	Slang Term	What It Means
Awesome	very great	No problem	do not worry about it
All right!	very good	No way	I do not believe it or I am surprised
Cool	really interesting	OK (okay)	yes, or all right
Forget it	it is not important	Shut up	be quiet
Great	very good	U'huh	yes
Gross	something disgusting	Weird	strange, bizarre
Just kidding	I did not mean it	What's up?	what is going on?
Kinda	somewhat, a little bit	Wow	really great
Never mind	it is not important	Yea	yes

Jargon

The meaning of words also changes depending on the place they are spoken. **Jargon** is words used by a specific group of people or in a specific work setting. For example, people who work with computers might say "hardware" to mean electronic pieces of the equipment inside the computer. You may hear the same term "hardware" on a construction site to mean a hammer or nails. It can take time to fully understand the various jargon commonly used in American conversations. Do not be afraid to ask someone to what he or she is referring.

American English speakers also use words and expressions from books, TV, magazines, other cultures, and the jargon we encounter every day. Our language is always changing. Words go in and out of style like clothing! For example, if you are in a meeting and someone says to you, "Let's take this offline," they mean they want to have a private conversation with you. This particular phrase was first used on Internet chat sessions. Do not be afraid to ask what someone means.

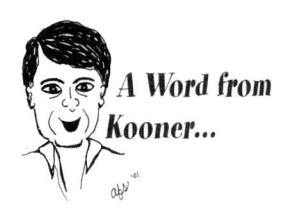

A Word from Kooner...

Here are some helpful hints for communicating...

- Talk slowly but clearly
- Explain things as well as you can even if you have to write it down
- If you are not clear about a name, ask someone to spell it
- Spell it for them if you have to
- Use this method when you spell – 'M' like Mary. 'P' like Paul, etc.
- Listening is a good thing
- Think before you say it
- Translate in your own head before you speak
- Always listen to new words and use them
- Just ask – What does it mean? Can you explain?
- Learn some dialogues from TV or radio
- Learn the polite way to say certain things and use them...(this is a big one)
- Spell your name over the phone if you have to
- You can ask to repeat information from other individuals if you are not clear
- Make dialogues with simple English until you learn more
- Learn when to say I am sorry, thank you, and when to apologize
- Relax...knowing your mother language does not make you less smart.

Speaking the Language

Trying to speak English is one of the best things you can do to help you learn. When you are starting to speak English, try to:

- **Keep it simple** – Do not try to add too many difficult words at one time. Use words you are comfortable with. Use a dictionary if necessary.
- **Speak as slowly as you need** – Try to relax and speak at a pace that is comfortable. If you get nervous and rush, the person you are speaking to may have trouble understanding what you are saying.
- **Speak clearly** – Avoid talking so softly that others cannot understand you.

It is important to keep practicing. Do not get frustrated. If you are not sure of a word, try to use pictures or items to show what you are trying to say.

Listening

Listening is an important part of communication and is a great way to improve your speaking. You can learn new words and better understand words you already know. You must be patient and focused on the speaker to be a good listener.

Sometimes words or phrases mean different things to different people. To help you understand what is being said, try to:

- **Ask Questions** – Do not be afraid to ask questions when you do not understand. The more questions you ask, the faster you can learn the language.
- **Repeat or Restate** – When someone is speaking to you, repeat what you think you heard in your own words when they are finished. This will help the speaker know if you understood.

Immigrant Views

"When I took my driver's license test in English, I failed by one question. When they gave me a translation, I got 100% the same day. From that day I knew how important it was to learn English."

Maria Juarez, Immigrated from Mexico in 1999

Nonverbal Communication

Actions and gestures are an important part of communication. The way we dress, stand, look at others, and use our voices sometimes communicate more to people than what words we choose. In the United States, there is a saying: "It is not '*what*' we say, but '*how*' we say it that really matters."

For example, if you wanted to get to know one of your co-workers, what would you do? If you walk up to them with a smile and extend your hand, you will appear friendly. If you are slumped over and without a smile, they may think you are unfriendly or unhappy.

Gestures

Gestures are the movements you make with your arms and hands while speaking. For example, waving your hand means "hello" whether you actually say "hello" or not! Gestures can help reinforce what is being said.

There are many gestures that are similar throughout the world. A wave, or putting your hand up to say "stop" are a couple of examples. There are also gestures specific to one country or one place. Sometimes gestures with a positive meaning in one country can be insulting in another country. It is important to remember this during conversations so you do not offend anyone or become offended yourself. If you are not sure what a person means by a gesture they make, ask them.

"Thumb's up" means good, OK, or go.

Body Movement and Posture

How we stand, walk, sit, and use our hands helps tell people what we feel and think. If we stand up straight with our shoulders square, it means we are confident. If we slouch, people may think we do not care or are tired.

When you are at work, for example, if you always sit alone in a corner in the break room, people may think you are unfriendly or do not want to talk to anyone. If you are always looking down when you talk, or rock back and forth on your feet, Americans may think you are nervous or afraid. When you are communicating with people, be aware of how you are standing and what message you are sending with your body!

Space

When we talk about "space" and gestures, we are talking about **personal space,** the actual physical space between people. In every country, people are brought up with different beliefs and standards. How close you stand, how much you should touch others, and how you greet people may be different. In America, it is normal to keep about 18 inches (.45 m.) between you and unfamiliar people. If you stand too close, it may make people uncomfortable.

Facial Expressions and Eye Contact

Facial expressions can tell someone if you are sad, happy, angry, or confused. It is important to remember in some countries, the workplace is very serious. In America, not only is it appropriate to smile in the workplace, it is expected!

Americans like about 18 inches (.45 m.) between themselves and people they do not know.

Eye contact is important when interacting with others. In America, direct eye contact is expected. In other countries, direct eye contact may be seen as a sign of disrespect. If you do not use direct eye contact, people may think you are not telling the truth or you do not believe in what you are saying.

What your Face May be Telling Someone...

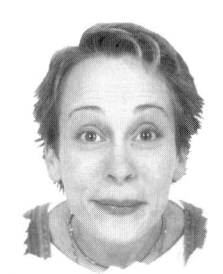

I'm listening to you
That's great!

I don't believe that
I don't trust it

I'm tired, I'm bored
I'm thinking about something else

I'm not sure
I'm nervous

Remember, while you do want to use direct eye contact, you do not want to make people feel that you are staring at them.

Using Your Voice

Another way you communicate without words is how you use your voice. How loud, soft, fast, or slow you speak can tell the listener how you feel. Your voice can show nervousness, excitement, or confusion. Sometimes when people get excited, they talk in high, shrill voices. If they are sad or angry, they may talk in a lower voice.

It is very important to remember in a U.S. workplace, you should not show extreme emotion in front of co-workers or customers. If you are angry or upset, you need to be calm and not let the customer see you angry.

Clothing

Your clothing and appearance are powerful forms of nonverbal communication. If your clothes are wrinkled and your hair is messy, people may think you are lazy. If you wear too much jewelry, people might think you are trying to draw attention to yourself. The next chapter discusses hygiene and dress in more detail.

Touch

People react differently to touch – a hug, a kiss, a handshake, a pat on the back, or a touch on the shoulder can mean different things in different settings. The situation or your family background impact how you view touch. Americans' comfort levels with touch will vary based on background and the region of the country. Generally, it is polite not to touch people you do not know.

Some cultures have unwritten rules that dictate when it is OK to touch. For example, in Europe you may see two people greet each other with a hug and a kiss on the cheek. In the United States, people usually greet each other with a handshake. In America, kissing and hugging are usually reserved for personal relationships.

A handshake is a common greeting.

Summary

Learning American English is one of the most important things you can do for your success. There are many ways to learn and practice the language every day. It is also important to remember it is not just what you say, but how you say it. How you use your body and how you dress affect how people react to you. Communicating effectively can open opportunities, build friendships and give a sense of pride.

Resources

Website

http://www/esl-lab.com—ESL Lab.

Glossary

ESL: English as a Second Language.

Gestures: movements you make with your arms and hands while speaking.

Jargon: words used by a specific group of people or in a specific work setting.

Personal Space: the actual physical space between people.

Slang: a casual word or expression.

Vocabulary: the number of words you know.

Exercises

1. Internet Exercise (see Pages 211-212 for more information on the Internet): Log on to any search engine (www.google.com, www.dogpile.com, www.yahoo.com) and search by the following terms to learn more about the English language:

   - English as a second language
   - How to learn English
   - Phonics
   - Exercises in speaking English
   - American slang
   - American jargon
   - Gestures
   - Posture
   - Personal space

Exercises

2. Take the evening off and invite a friend or two to watch a movie or television program.
   - Each of you should make a list of 10 to 20 words you do not understand (help each other to spell words on your list).
   - When the program is over, share your lists with each other and guess what each word means.
   - After you have taken a guess at what each word means, look them up in the dictionary or on the Internet (www.dictionary.com is a popular site).

   You may be surprised at how many meanings one word can have!

CHAPTER 4

HYGIENE, GROOMING, AND CLOTHING

To be successful in the United States, it is important to have a clean body and an orderly appearance. Your clothing should always be neat, clean, and appropriate. Americans are sometimes accused of being obsessed with cleanliness. To someone in the United States, being clean means having no stains, dirt, sweat, or body odor. Cleanliness also includes having clean hair, fingernails, and clothes. Freshly washed and pressed clothing shows others you are professional and ready to succeed.

Sanitation and grooming standards vary among countries. Please do not be offended if it seems information in this chapter is at a basic level. Please take what you need from the information provided.

Note to the Mentor

How to use an American bathroom should be addressed as soon as possible. Facilities and products can differ from country to country. Acquaint the immigrant with the basics of using public toilets and private restrooms, washing hands, bathing, and brushing teeth. Be open and honest about the process. This is one area where a lack of knowledge can be more embarrassing than talking about the subject! You should also make sure he or she knows about all the hygiene and toiletry products available in the United States.

IN THIS CHAPTER
- Sanitation facilities in the United States
- Cleanliness standards
- Personal grooming
- Wearing jewelry at work
- Clothing for work
- Casual clothing
- Personal services

Sanitation and Hygiene

Toilet Facilities

Let us look at the average American **restroom**, or toilet facilities. In most public buildings, men and women have separate restrooms. Some buildings do have a single restroom unit that can be used by men or women. Public restrooms are often built so people with disabilities can use the facility more easily.

Common Words for Toilet Facilities:	For Men
✦ Restroom	✦ Men's room
✦ Bathroom	✦ Gentlemen
✦ The head (military use)	✦ Little boy's room
✦ The john	**For Women**
✦ Potty	✦ Ladies' room
	✦ Ladies
Americans usually do not say "Where is the toilet?" They will say, "Where is the **restroom**?"	✦ Powder room
	✦ Little girl's room
	✦ Women's lounge

Here are some words used in the U.S. to describe urination and bowel movements:

Urinate		Defecate/ Bowel Movement	
Piss *	Potty	Shit*	Potty
Pee	Whizz	Poop	Take a dump*

* These terms are slang some people find offensive! Most Americans say, "I need to use the restroom."

American restrooms contain individual stalls with a toilet in each stall for privacy. Most toilets have a seat to sit on. Some stalls have dispensers with disposable paper seat covers you can place on the seat to help protect you from bacteria. Paper seat covers are flushed down the toilet when you are finished.

Toilet Stall

Toilets may have a handle or lever. This handle is pushed down to flush the toilet. Some toilets have a button on the wall to press

Sanitation and Hygiene

Toilet Paper

that flushes the toilet. Other toilets have an electronic sensor that automatically flushes the toilet when you stand up or leave the stall.

Each stall contains **toilet paper,** a thin, absorbent paper on a roll. Toilet paper is used to clean yourself after a bowel movement or urination.

In many women's restrooms, stalls will have a special container to place used **feminine hygiene products**. Feminine hygiene products are maxi pads, sanitary napkins, and tampons used during menstrual cycles. Tampons are the only feminine hygiene product that should be placed in a toilet. Some women's restrooms have vending machines where you can purchase individual hygiene products. Feminine hygiene products are discussed in more detail later in this chapter.

Public men's restrooms may look very different from the women's restrooms. In men's restrooms, toilet stalls are usually used for bowel movements. The stalls may be open. Public men's restrooms also contain **urinals**. Urinals are used only for urination. Urinals are flushed in the same way as toilets. Urinals will often have a urinal cake, or deodorizer, to help keep the restroom smelling clean. There are very few women's urinals in the United States. Female urinals are not sat upon.

Urinal

Washing Your Hands

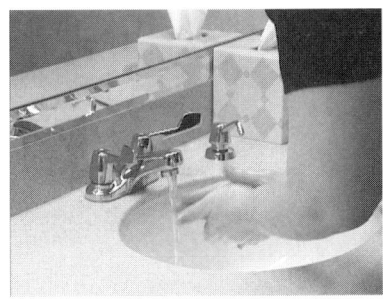

Hand-washing Sink

After using a toilet or urinal, you should always wash your hands. Washing your hands helps to prevent the spread of germs and disease. Use a sink to wash your hands with soap and warm water. Soap is available in a dispenser. Soap dispensers are found next to the sink or on the wall in front of the sink.

If the sink has two handles, the **hot water is on the left** and the **cold water is on the right**. The sink may only have one handle to control the faucet. Turning the handle to the left will make the water hot. Turning the handle to the right will make the water cold. Some sinks have handles that are pressed down instead of turning. The water will stop after several seconds. A few sinks do not have any handles. These sinks use a motion sensor. Just place your hands under the faucet and the water will come on. When you are finished rinsing your hands, pull your hands out from under the faucet and the water will stop.

Drying Your Hands

Public restrooms offer two main ways of drying your hands—paper towels or electric hand dryers. Paper towel dispensers are located on the wall near the sinks. Place any paper towels you may have used in the trash can. Many bathrooms have electric hand dryers. Push the button on the dryer, and hot air will come out of the vent. Rub your hands together in the heated air to dry your hands.

Hand Dryer

The following pictures show how to wash and dry your hands. Follow these steps to have hands that are properly clean and free of germs:

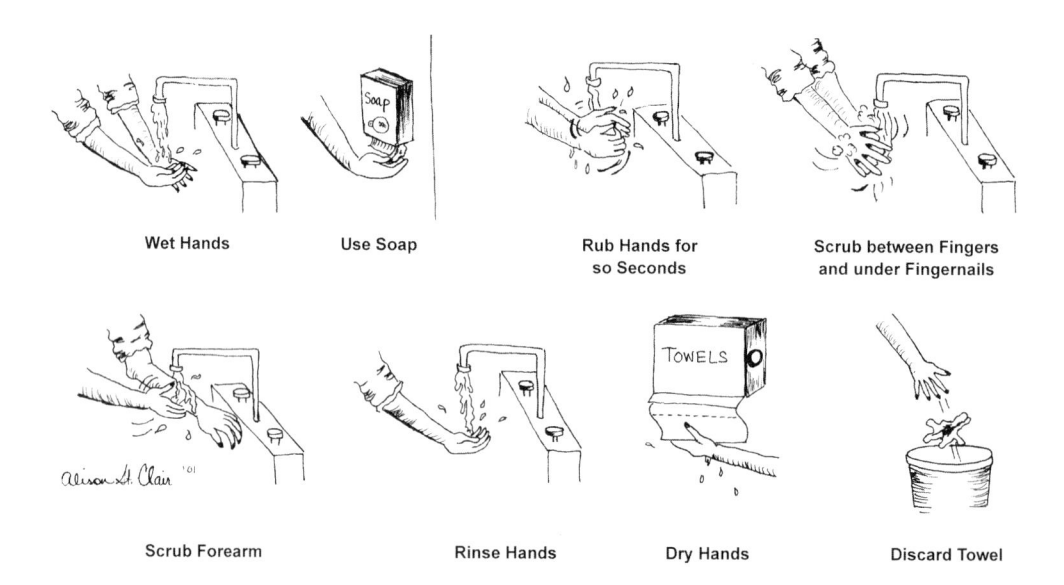

| Wet Hands | Use Soap | Rub Hands for
so Seconds | Scrub between Fingers and under Fingernails |

| Scrub Forearm | Rinse Hands | Dry Hands | Discard Towel |

Step-by-Step Hand-washing Procedure

Physically Disabled Access

Every public restroom should have one stall larger than the other stalls. This special stall is designed for people who are physically disabled. These stalls have higher toilets. The stall will have handrails on the walls. The stalls are large enough to accommodate a wheelchair or scooter.

This sign shows wheelchair accessibility.

Baby-Changing Stations

Many public restrooms contain changing tables. Most changing tables fold down from the wall. The table can be used to change a baby or young child's diaper. Sometimes changing tables are located in the largest stall in the restroom. Recently, they have become more common in men's rooms, as well.

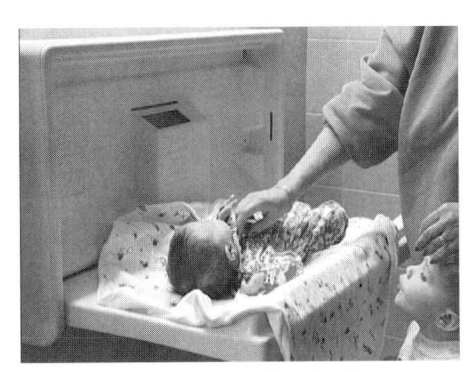

Baby-Changing Station

Feminine Hygiene

Women who are menstruating can find sanitary products in the **feminine hygiene** section of a store. Most U.S. women use **sanitary pads** or **tampons**. Pads are made of cotton or other absorbent materials. They may have a thin plastic layer to prevent leaks. They are made in many different sizes and shapes. Some pads have adhesive flaps on the sides to help them stay in place.

Tampons are small rolls of absorbent material that are inserted into the vagina to absorb menstrual flow. Tampons are made in different absorbencies and may come in applicators to make them easy to insert. Applicators are thrown away after you have inserted the tampon. Tampons are removed by pulling on the strings attached to the tampon. The strings should hang outside the body after you insert the tampon. It is very important to change your tampon at least every four to eight hours. See usage instructions on tampon packages for more information. Tampons may be flushed in a toilet. Pads should be disposed of in the container in the restroom stall.

Safer Sex

People want to protect themselves from **sexually transmitted diseases (STDs)** such as HIV or AIDS. Using latex **condoms** during sexual activity can help reduce the transmission of most STDs. The condom is utilized to keep body fluids from being exchanged. Condoms are available in many stores, near the feminine hygiene section. Talk to a doctor if you need more information on STD prevention.

Hygiene—Keeping Clean

Americans are very concerned about cleanliness. We have excellent sanitation all over the country. Running water and toilets are available in most homes and buildings. Showering or bathing daily is a common practice in the United States. People in the United States see bathing as an important way to keep clean and free of disease.

It is important to know **Americans are very sensitive to body odor**. People in the United States find natural body odors offensive. A person who has strong body odor or whose hair seems greasy or unwashed is usually avoided.

Bathing/Showering

Take a shower or bath with soap and warm water every day. Most apartments and homes have a bathtub. Usually, the bathtub will also include a shower. Some apartments may not have a bathtub and will only have a shower stall. Most Americans take showers every day. Showers take less time than a bath. Some people feel it is easier to wash their hair in a shower. Many Americans view baths as a special chance to relax.

In the United States, you can find many varieties and scents of soap. You can find hard bars of soap. You can also find liquid soaps and bath gels which are applied with a washcloth or a mesh sponge. There are special soaps for sensitive skin, dry skin, oily skin, and other soaps are scented. Choose a product you like. Americans also like to use special soaps and cleansers on their faces. These cleansers may help heal or prevent blemishes, add moisture, or remove oil, dirt, and makeup.

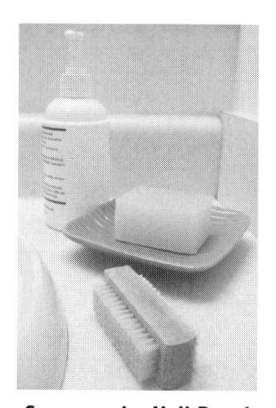

Soaps and a Nail Brush

Washing Your Hair

Shampoo is soap for your hair. There are many different products available for different types of hair. Read the label on the bottle to decide what shampoo is best for you. **Conditioner** helps soften and untangle hair. Some people never use conditioner. Other people use conditioner every day.

You can buy many specialized hair care products to help maintain and style your hair. If you have **dandruff** (flakes of dead skin in your hair) you can use a medicated shampoo to control it. If you choose to use oil in your hair, use only a small amount. Your hair should not appear to be greasy.

Hands and Fingernails

Make sure to clean underneath your fingernails. A fingernail brush can help you remove dirt from under your nails. If you have a job where your hands get very dirty, you may need to use a special soap to remove grease or other difficult stains. Purchase a nail care kit that includes nail clippers and a nail file. In the United States, it is important to keep your nails well-groomed and trimmed. Your hands will be one of the first things people see when they shake hands with you.

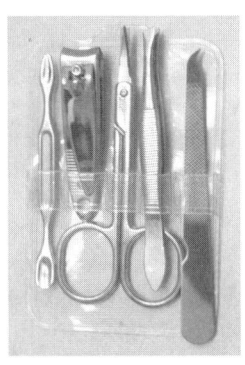

Nail Care Kit

After Bathing

After bathing, use a **deodorant** or **antiperspirant** under your arms to prevent odor. Antiperspirants control sweat, and deodorants control odor. Many products are both a deodorant and an antiperspirant. These products are only applied under the arm. There are special deodorant sprays and powders you can buy to use on your feet or elsewhere on your body. Some people also use moisturizers. Moisturizers are oils or creams that soften and protect skin. Some moisturizers can protect you from overexposure to the sun. You can also use talcum powders, sometimes called baby powder, to prevent odor.

Perfume and Cologne

Americans are also very sensitive to perfumes and colognes. Some people can have allergic reactions to perfume and cologne. If you wish to wear a perfume or cologne, apply only a very small amount. You do not want people to smell it from a distance. Most importantly, **do not use perfume or cologne to hide strong body odor**! If you have strong body odor, take a shower or bath.

If you enjoy eating lots of garlic or onions, your body may release these odors through your skin. You may find it helpful to eat less of these foods if you are having trouble with body odor.

Body Hair

For Women: In the United States, it is common for women to shave the hair from under their arms and on their legs. In the U.S. workplace, it is generally considered unacceptable for women to reveal legs that are unshaven. If a woman does not want to shave her legs, she might choose clothing that covers her legs, such as slacks or long dresses and skirts. You will find many products and methods for hair removal available in stores including razors, shaving cream or soap, and hair removal creams.

For Men: Facial hair is acceptable in the form of mustaches, beards, goatees, and sideburns. Facial hair should be neatly maintained and groomed. If a man prefers not to have facial hair, he would need to shave daily. Facial stubble is not considered professional. Some industries do not allow men to have long hair or facial hair. Ask your employer if your company has any special rules about facial hair.

Well-Groomed Facial Hair

Mouth Care

Having breath odor is as offensive to Americans as body odor. Breath odor can come from the foods you eat—such as garlic, onions, or spices. Oral hygiene is very important in the United States. You should brush your teeth with toothpaste at least once daily. Many Americans feel it is important to brush teeth twice a day. Some even brush their teeth after every meal or snack! There are many kinds of **toothbrushes** you can use to keep your teeth clean. **Dental floss** is coated string used to clean between teeth. There are also many kinds of toothpastes, dental flosses, and products that can help to control breath odor.

Toothbrush, Toothpaste, and Dental Floss

Mouthwash is a liquid rinse used after brushing that may kill germs in the mouth and freshen breath. Some mouthwashes only cover the odor, but others are medicated to kill germs and bacteria. Be sure to read the label. Do not use mouthwash as a replacement for brushing teeth. It is used after brushing your teeth. Swish the mouthwash around in your mouth and then spit it out in the sink. Do not be afraid to ask a friend to tell you if your breath or body odors are strong. It can be difficult to notice your own odors.

Many restaurants offer free peppermint candy at the checkout counter. Use these to freshen your breath after eating. People also chew gum to remove food from teeth after eating. Some people use toothpicks to remove food from between teeth.

Peppermint candies help freshen breath.

Hygiene products are a big business in America. Companies spend millions of dollars a year to get us to buy their products. Some products are sold for women, others for men, and some are for both sexes.

> ### Key Points to Keeping Clean:
>
> - A clean body is expected.
> - If you have body odor, take a bath or shower. If you cannot tell, get into the habit of bathing daily.
> - Wash your hair frequently and keep it clean.
> - Too much perfume or cologne is considered offensive.
>
> **Americans are very sensitive to body odor!**

Grooming—How You Look

Being clean is just the first step of good grooming. Looking neat, with your hair styled and your clothes pressed and clean, is also important.

Hair

Make sure your hair is neatly styled. Your hair can be long or short, braided, straight, or curly. What is important is that your hair is clean. Hair should be managed so your eyes can be seen and does not interfere with your job. Keep your hair combed or brushed. A good haircut is the best way to keep your hair looking neat. Most Americans have their hair cut by a stylist or barber on a regular basis. Some Americans prefer a short style because it is easier to care for and style.

Keep your hair neat and clean.

Jewelry

Jewelry is very personal. If you want to look professional, it is always better to wear less jewelry. Wearing too much jewelry or jewelry that is large may be considered inappropriate. Men in the United States typically do not wear much jewelry. Keep your display of jewelry simple. Be cautious of wearing expensive jewelry. When in doubt, do not wear it. Your employer may have certain requirements for jewelry and your appearance on the job. Check in your employee handbook to see what is allowed.

Employer Regulations for Jewelry—Many employers restrict the types of jewelry you can wear on the job for safety reasons. Jewelry can get caught in machinery or fall into food or supplies. In many restaurant and factory jobs, you are limited to very little jewelry. A watch, a ring on each hand and a pair of small earrings are common limits for jewelry. Some employers ask you to not wear bracelets or clusters of large earrings. Some may not want you to wear more than one earring on each ear. Some employers will not allow men to wear any earrings.

If you are uncertain as to what is allowed, read the employee handbook. Look at the jewelry other people are wearing on the job. A good rule to follow is to wear no more than one ring on each hand, simple earrings, and a bracelet or watch.

For Men: Most men wear very little jewelry. Common jewelry includes a **wristwatch** and a **wedding ring** worn on the left hand.
Some men also wear:

- An **additional ring** on the other hand.
- A **metal bracelet** on wrist opposite the watch.
- **Earring(s)**—Some men have pierced one or both ears. Men usually wear a stud earring. Stud earrings are simple earrings that do not stick out far from the earlobe or have any part that dangles.
- **Chains**—A simple chain is better than a heavy chain. Men who wear several heavy chains may be seen as unprofessional.

Common Jewelry for Men

For Women: Wearing less jewelry is always better than wearing too much. Common jewelry for women includes:

- **Wristwatch.**
- **Wedding ring** worn on the left hand. An engagement ring may also be worn.
- **Additional ring** on the other hand. Try to limit the number of rings on your hands to only one ring.
- **Earrings** – usually one per ear. Some women have multiple pierces and they wear post or stud earrings in the other holes.
- **Chain/pendant.**
- **Bracelet**.

Common Jewelry for Women

Body Piercing

Many companies have a policy of only one piercing per ear. Piercing of the eyebrow, nose or tongue may not be allowed by your employer. If you have a religious reason for a facial piercing, explain your reasons to your employer. You may be asked to cover the opening or not wear jewelry in it during work time.

Check your company policy on body piercing and tattoos.

Tattoos

Some companies may not allow visible tattoos. You may need to cover the tattoo with makeup. Do not be surprised if you are asked this question during an interview. Again, if you have a religious reason for the tattoo, discuss it with your manager.

Clothing

What you are wearing and how you look will affect how people treat you. Wearing the right clothing for the right occasion will help you make a good impression on others. If your shirt is wrinkled or stained, others may think you are careless or irresponsible.

Dressing for the Job

Your clothes can help make you successful. Inappropriate clothes can cause problems for you. If you are working in an office setting, you may be required to dress formally. Appropriate clothes for office work can mean a suit and tie for a man, or a suit, dress, or pantsuit for a woman.

People in the United States like to be comfortable at work. Some companies are allowing a more casual environment. Many offices have a "dress–down" day on Fridays. These Fridays are days where people wear more casual business clothes. Other offices will allow you to wear business casual clothes every day. Still other offices are very casual, with no requirements at all for dress.

Dress properly for the workplace.

Finally, there are many jobs and professions that require you to wear a uniform. If this is the case, it is important you wear the entire uniform while at work. Check with your employer to learn about dress requirements.

Inappropriate Clothing

At work, you should not wear clothing that reveals too much of your body. If you are a woman, wearing dresses that are very short or that reveal part of your bosom are inappropriate. For men, tight pants or a shirt that is unbuttoned by more than one or two buttons is inappropriate.

When you are building your professional wardrobe, keep in mind fashions change on a seasonal basis. Try to purchase outfits that can be worn comfortably all year-round. This means the outfit should be appropriate for cold and warm weather and should have a simple style. Hemlines for women's skirts and dresses are generally at, or slightly above, the knee. Miniskirts or very short skirts are not acceptable in business.

Interviewing for a Job

When interviewing for a job, it is important to dress more formally than the position you are applying for. If you are a man applying for an office position, you should probably wear a suit and tie. If you are a woman applying for an office position, wear a suit or dress. If you are applying for a labor or service position, a suit may be too formal. A more casual appearance, such as slacks and a shirt, may be appropriate. You should never wear jeans and a T-shirt to an interview. If you look messy, an employer may think your work will be messy, too. It is better to be too formal than too casually dressed for an interview.

Make a good impression with your clothing.

Take Care of Your Clothes

Clean - Make sure your clothes are clean every day. You should not wear the same clothing two days in a row. This is especially true of your socks and underwear.

No Wrinkles - You should wear clothing that has no wrinkles. You can buy clothes that are wrinkle resistant. Some people who dress formally at work use a cleaning service to clean and press their clothes each week.

Dry Cleaning - If you purchase clothes labeled "Dry Clean Only," do not wash them at home. You need to take them to a **dry cleaners**.

Uniforms - If you wear a uniform at work, you may be given several uniforms. You may need to wash your uniform yourself, or your employer may collect and clean your uniforms each week.

Keep clothes neat and clean.

Clothing

Proper Fit - Properly fitting clothing has become very important for safety reasons. Clothing that is too big can be caught in equipment. Clothing that is too tight can be inappropriate.

Colors - Depending on the region of the country, some colors may be more appropriate than others. People living in warmer regions of the country tend to wear lighter colored clothing all year. People in cooler climates tend to wear darker colors. A suit that is appropriate in Arizona, which is a very warm and dry state, may not be appropriate in New York, which is a cooler and wet state.

Casual Clothing - Comfortable clothing is worn by most people when they are not working. Common choices for men and women include:

- T-shirt
- Polo shirt
- Jeans
- Shorts
- Sweat shirt and sweat pants
- Tennis shoes (athletic shoes)
- Sandals

Business/ Formal Clothing - Many people, especially in an office, wear more formal clothing at work.

Men
- Suit coat and matching pants
- **Sports coat**
- Trousers
- Button-down shirt
- Necktie
- **Dress shoes**

Women
- Suit - Jacket with matching pants or skirt
- Skirt and blouse
- Dress
- Blouse with pants
- **Stockings or hose**
- Dress shoes

Business Casual Clothing - Many people can wear work clothes that are more relaxed than a suit or dress. Common choices for men and women include:

- **Polo shirt**
- Sports shirt
- **Khakis** or casual pants (not jeans)
- Casual shoes (not athletic shoes or sandals)

Strange Things in American English...

The word **"dress"** has several meanings. It can mean:

- To put clothes on (I am getting **dressed** for work.)
- A woman's garment (She was wearing a beautiful **dress**.)
- To wear clothes of a certain style (The people at the party were casually **dressed**.)
- To be attired more formally (Mary's shoes were very **dressy**.).

Shoes

Your shoes are an important part of your outfit. You need to wear shoes appropriate for your job. Your employer may require you to wear a special shoe with a steel toe for construction work, or non-slip shoes when working in a kitchen. If in doubt, ask your supervisor for advice. Keep your shoes polished and clean. Your shoes should coordinate with the rest of your outfit. Make sure your socks also match the clothes you wear.

No Shoes, No Shirt, No Service

Many stores have a policy that you must wear shoes, pants, and a shirt in their shop. They can refuse to sell you anything and can ask you to leave if you do not do this. You often see this sign in a window or on a door to the shop.

Many of the same rules that apply for work, apply for going out in public. How you dress, regardless of where you are, determines what people are going to think. You always want to be at your best!

Personal Services

In America, there are many businesses that provide personal services. For example, there are many choices when it comes to taking care of your hair. You may want to have a haircut or have your hair colored or styled. Barber shops generally cut men's hair only. Styling salons work with both men's and women's hair. Most of these businesses require you to call and make an appointment to come in. Many of these shops can also give you a massage, a manicure, or a pedicure. There are other shops which cut hair, where you can walk in without an appointment. These places typically offer limited services. Day spas offer services that range from facials, to massages, to any care for your hair and body.

What are tennis shoes?

Tennis shoes are a term we use for all kinds of athletic shoes. Running shoes, walking shoes, cross trainers (used for running or sports), basketball shoes, etc.... are all called tennis shoes.

Dress Up for Better Service...

You may find in America if you go to a nice store in nice clothes, you will have better service and be treated better by the staff. If you go into a nice store in very casual or dirty clothes, salespeople may think you do not have the money to spend or you may be trying to steal from them. Your service will not be as good, and people will be less friendly and willing to give you help.

Summary

Maintaining proper grooming can be a lot of work. By being well-groomed and dressed appropriately, you can be more successful in your job and be able to advance your career. Wear appropriate clothing that is neat and clean. Being well-groomed and neatly dressed brings benefits off the job as well. You will find people around you respond more positively to you when you are well-groomed.

Glossary

Antiperspirant: cream or spray applied under the armpit to control sweat.

Baby-changing stations: changing tables usually hang on a wall and fold down from the wall. The table can be used to change a baby or young child's diaper.

Business casual: more casual dress for work than a suit and tie. No suit, no tie, long pressed pants, not jeans, collared shirt for a man. A woman may vary her appearance with a skirt, casual shirt or blouse, typically wearing low-heeled shoes.

Conditioner: liquid used after shampoo to soften and untangle hair.

Condom: a form-fitting piece of latex designed to cover an erect penis. It is utilized to retain the sperm and keep body fluids from being exchanged. Condoms help minimize sexually transmitted diseases and pregnancy.

Dandruff: flakes of dead skin in your hair.

Dental floss: coated string used to clean between teeth.

Deodorant: cream or spray applied under the armpit to control odor.

Dress shoes: a polished shoe, coordinated with the pants, skirt or suit being worn by the person.

Dry cleaning: a chemical process for cleaning and pressing clothes that does not use water. Done by professionals in this service field.

Feminine hygiene products: maxi pads, sanitary napkins, and tampons used during menstrual cycles.

Khakis: pants in solid colors that are for casual or business casual wear. They are more formal than jeans and less formal than dress pants, and worn by both men and women.

Monogamous: The practice of being sexually intimate with only one other person.

Mouthwash: a liquid rinse used after brushing your teeth that will freshen breath and may kill germs in the mouth.

Restroom: toilet facilities.

Panty hose: also known as nylons, hose or stockings that a woman wears over her legs, typically one piece. They range in colors from skin tones to white, navy, and black.

Polo shirt: a collared knit shirt, usually short sleeved. Many companies will have their logos sewn onto the shirt.

Sanitary pads: pads made of cotton or other absorbent materials used to control menstruation. They may have a thin plastic layer to prevent leaks. They are made in many different sizes and shapes.

Sexually transmitted diseases (STDs): diseases people get with unprotected sexual contact.

Shampoo: liquid soap designed for your hair.

Sports jacket: also known as a sports coat, it is a jacket not made of the same color and fabric as the trousers/pants. A tie may or may not be required to complete the outfit. (See photo in Business/Formal page 47.)

Tampons: small rolls of absorbent material inserted into the vagina to absorb menstrual flow. Most tampons come in applicators to make them easy to insert. Tampons are removed by pulling on the strings attached to the tampon. See usage instructions on tampon packages for more information.

Toilet paper: thin, absorbent paper usually in a roll. Toilet paper is used to clean yourself after a bowel movement or urination.

Toothpaste: a cleaner used on a brush to clean teeth.

Urinals: wall-mounted ceramic basins flushed with water that men use while standing up to urinate.

Exercises

1. Internet Exercise (see Pages 209-210 for more information on the Internet): Log onto any search engine (www.google.com, www.dogpile.com, www.yahoo.com) and search by the following terms to learn more about personal hygiene, grooming and dress:
   - Proper personal hygiene
   - Personal hygiene products
   - Feminine hygiene
   - Safe sex
   - Monogamy
   - Planned parenthood
   - Sexually transmitted diseases
   - Personal sanitation
   - Personal grooming
   - Business attire.

2. There are many types of personal hygiene products (deodorant, hair spray, shampoo, etc . . .) that do many different things. Each type of product can be sold under several different names. For example, deodorants can be spray, roll-on, or stick, and several companies can sell each kind.

   Name brands are typically more expensive than the generic brands, and they usually do the same thing. Try this exercise to become a more informed consumer.

   - Pick two types of personal hygiene products (shampoo and bar soap for example) you know very little about or want to know more about.
   - You and your friend buy the generic (store brand) and a name brand (Pert® and Dial®) of each product.
   - Each of you use the generic product for a week and the name brand product during the next week.
   - Sit down with your friend and talk about the differences you have experienced with the products.

   You decide if they live up to what they promise!

Chapter 5

Cash and Credit

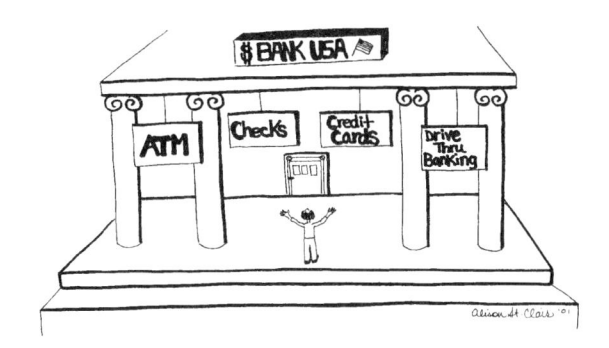

It is very important to have enough money to do what you want for yourself and your family. Money can help you find a better way of living and improve your life. We will take a look at the basics of banking, savings, investments, and credit cards in this chapter.

Now you are in America, it is important to learn to use American currency. It will also be helpful to understand the nation's banking system. There are many different ways to buy things, pay for services, pay bills, and invest your money. Many businesses and banks offer credit cards, that allow you to buy an item now and pay for it at a later time, or over a period of time. Many Americans take advantage of credit.

Cash/Currency

The main unit of U.S. currency is the **dollar**. U.S. currency comes in bills (paper form) and coins. Bills and coins come in many different values. There are 100 cents to a dollar. Thinking in terms of U.S. dollars and not in the currency of your home country can be a challenge! Another name for currency is **cash**. Cash is the most commonly accepted form of payment at stores. Some stores will only accept cash. It is the most common form of payment to use when paying for lower cost items. Using cash is a good way to begin to understand the value of American money.

In This Chapter

- U.S. currency
- Using cash for purchases
- Setting up bank accounts
- Using checks
- Credit cards
- Investments
- Retirement accounts

Banks and Bank Accounts

Many people choose to put their money in a bank for safety and to invest their money. There are many banks in the United States. There are different types of accounts you can open with a bank. You may be able to open a checking account, savings account, or an investment account. Having an account with a bank allows you to cash paychecks easily.

To open an account, you need a photo ID, proof of your address, and a social security number.

No matter what bank you use, be sure the bank is federally insured. You may see a sticker on the doors or windows of the bank that reads "Member FDIC." FDIC (Federal Depository Insurance Corporation) is the most common form of federal insurance. This means if the bank closes permanently for any reason or if the bank is robbed, the federal government would provide the money for customers to be paid.

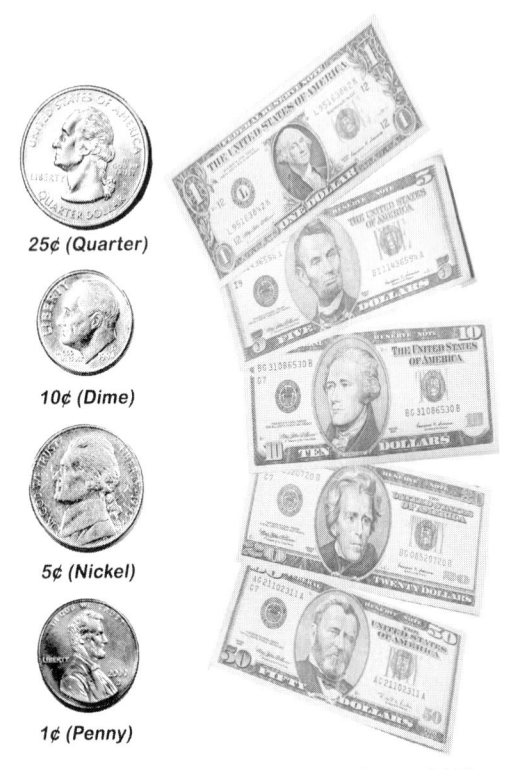

25¢ (Quarter)
10¢ (Dime)
5¢ (Nickel)
1¢ (Penny)

American currency comes in coins and bills.

Bank Services

Banks provide many services, such as the ability to do banking over the phone, the Internet, or at an ATM.

ATM Machines—An **ATM (Automatic Teller Machine)** is a machine that provides basic banking services electronically 24 hours a day. You can make deposits, withdrawals, transfer money, pay bills, and print account statements with an ATM card at an ATM machine. Many people never even enter a bank after they open an account. Almost every bank has an ATM machine. Some banks have drive-through

People enjoy the convenience of ATMs.

ATMs so you do not even have to leave your car. Some stores, gas stations, and restaurants also have ATM machines.

Wire Transfers—If you are sending or receiving money from inside or outside the country, most banks allow electronic wire transfers to or from your account. An electronic transfer is when you move money from one account to another electronically. Banks usually charge a fee for this service.

Checking Accounts

The most common type of account at a bank is a **checking account**. With a checking account, you deposit your money with the bank and you write a check to take money out. When you want to purchase something or pay a debt, you can write a check for the amount from your checking account. A **check** is a paper that identifies you and your account and authorizes the payee to receive the amount you specify from your account. Banks will provide you with checks printed for you for a small fee. Most businesses accept checks as a form of payment and treat them like cash. In some stores you may need to show your driver's license or some other form of identification when you write a check.

Writing a check is an easy way to pay bills.

If you are sending a payment through the mail, you should pay with a check. Most companies will not accept cash as a payment through the mail for security reasons.

ATM Card—Many banks provide a plastic ATM card. An ATM card is a plastic card used at an automatic teller machine to do many basic banking features. ATM cards cannot be used in stores.

Debit Card—A debit card looks like a credit card or ATM card and can be used at a store like a credit card. Debit cards can also be used at ATM machines. Most places that accept credit cards also accept debit cards. Most will have signs near the register letting you know if they can accept debit cards.

A debit card acts like an electronic check. When you use a debit card to purchase something, the money for the purchase is automatically withdrawn directly from your checking account. If you try to buy something without enough money in your account, the debit card will be denied.

Savings Accounts

A **savings account** is a bank account you keep money in for a long period of time. Banks will pay you **interest** on money you deposit into savings accounts. Money can be transferred between accounts within the same bank. Many people choose to link their checking and savings accounts together. You can access your savings account from an ATM, so you can easily transfer money between your savings and checking accounts. Savings accounts usually have low interest rates.

Certificate of Deposits and Investments

If you have extra money you do not need to access for a period of time, you can make more money by opening a **certificate of deposit (CD)** account. You deposit your money with the bank for a certain length of time, and they pay you a set interest rate. The longer you deposit the money, the higher the rate. The drawback to CDs is you do not have access to the money. You pay large penalties if you withdraw the money early. One of the benefits is you can earn a higher interest rate than from a savings account.

Many banks offer additional investment opportunities. When you invest your money, you risk your money. You may gain large amounts of money, or you could lose large amounts of money. Usually the greater the financial risk, the higher the interest rate paid to you. Ask your bank about the **volatility**, or how risky, its investments are.

Loans and Mortgages

Most banks loan money to people. A **loan** is usually credit you receive from a bank, credit union, or loan company. You repay the loan over a period of time and pay interest on the loan. **Interest** is the fee paid to borrow money. Typically in the United States you would apply for a loan when buying a car or other expensive item. When considering a loan, the most important thing for you to do is compare interest rates. Interest rates can vary from one place to the other. An **interest rate** is the percentage the bank will charge you for borrowing the money. The lower the interest rate, the less you will have to pay for borrowing money.

When applying for a loan, the lender will look at:

- Your credit rating
- How long you have lived at your current address
- How long you have been employed

- How much you have "put down," or the percentage of the original purchase price you are paying up front.

If you have not established credit, you may have difficulty getting a loan. The best way to establish a credit history is to apply for a credit card. By using the credit card consistently and paying the monthly amount due on time, you can establish good credit.

Mortgages are a type of loan used for buying a house. Mortgages are paid back over a much longer period of time than many other kinds of loans. You may have as long as 30 years to pay off a mortgage. Read more about mortgages in Chapter 6, *Buying a House.*

Retirement Accounts

Most Americans save money each month for their **retirement,** the time when they are older and are no longer working. The federal government offers a program called social security to assist retired workers. Social security tax is taken out of each worker's paycheck. The money is invested by the government and is paid to workers over a certain age. You will be eligible to receive social security when you retire, but social security will not be able to pay for all your retirement.

Many banks have special accounts for retirement savings. One of the advantages of these accounts is the money is not taxable by the government until you reach a certain age. It is important to begin planning for your retirement as early as possible. The sooner you begin, the more money you will have when you retire.

Start saving for retirement early!

If your employer does not offer you a retirement account, it is important for you to start an account for yourself. Check with your local bank and financial investors.

Depositing Money in an Account

When you have a bank account you will find it easier to manage your money when you are paid.

Direct Deposit to Your Account—Some companies will automatically deposit your pay into your checking or savings account. This can give you access to your money more quickly and conveniently than by using a paper check. The company provides a form to fill out with information about your bank and bank account. This will provide you with immediate access to your money on payday. You still receive a pay stub showing the amount received and amount deducted for taxes and benefits. Direct deposit saves the employer time and money. Ask your employer if they offer direct deposit.

Cashing Your Check—If you decide you do not want to have your check automatically deposited, you will have to cash your check on payday. **Cashing** your check means going to the bank and depositing your check or exchanging your paycheck for currency.

Your paycheck can be cashed by a bank the check was issued from or where you have an account. Putting your money into a checking account will allow you access to your funds by writing a check or using a debit card. Some places, like fast-food restaurants, only accept cash. Other companies prefer a check or money order as methods of payment.

Credit Cards

Credit cards are a very popular and convenient way to purchase goods and services. A **credit card** is a plastic card you use instead of cash or a check to purchase items. A credit card represents a line of credit with a bank or credit company. Your agreement with the bank sets the limit to which you can charge purchases.

Before you can get a credit card, you need to be able to prove you have a job, a place to live, and a history of consistently paying your bills. You may be refused credit if you have too many debts, do not pay your bills regularly, or if you do not have enough credit history. Using a credit card wisely is a good way to build up your credit history.

Manage credit cards like cash.

Your Credit Rating

Your **credit rating,** or credit history, is a record of how well you pay your bills. Your credit may be checked when you apply for a job. Banks often check your rating when you open a bank account. You need to have a good credit rating if you want to buy a car or home. You can establish a good credit rating by paying your bills, credit cards, and loans on time.

Types of Credit Cards

There are many different choices of credit cards. The most common credit cards in the United States are:

- Visa
- MasterCard
- American Express
- Discover Card
- Diner's Club.

Most of these cards are accepted at any store around the country. Each store must pay a fee to accept these credit cards, so a business may choose to accept only certain cards.

Monthly and Revolving Charge Accounts

Most credit cards fall into two groups: monthly charge accounts and revolving charge accounts.

With **monthly charge accounts,** whatever money you charge for the month is due at the end of the next month. These cards usually do not charge any interest, but may have other fees for usage. American Express and Diner's Club are this type of credit card.

Revolving charge accounts require you to pay only a portion of your balance. With these accounts, you are charged interest for any unpaid amount carried forward to the next month. Interest rates can be high. This means you may pay large amounts of interest over time. Visa, MasterCard, and Discover are revolving charge accounts.

MasterCard and Visa—Different banks and different companies issue MasterCard and Visa cards. While each card is generally used the same in stores, payments and interest rates can be very different. When choosing a credit card, compare the interest rates being charged. Credit card companies are very competitive, so look for cards with the lowest interest rates. Interest rates can be between 2% and 26.99%!

Store Credit Cards—Many stores offer their own credit cards for purchases made at their store. Gas stations, department stores, hardware stores, and food stores offer credit cards. With some cards you may actually earn money for using their card for purchases.

Gold, Platinum, and Standard Cards

The salary you earn, how much credit you have, and how good your credit rating is will help determine the type of card you will receive. Always paying your bills on time may qualify you for a higher level of credit. Typically, gold and platinum cards have higher credit limits. Some companies also charge an annual fee. This means once a year you pay a set amount to continue using the card. Many companies do not have annual fees.

Secure Credit Cards

When you are first establishing credit or have had credit problems in the past, a credit card company may ask you to send them an amount of money which they then deposit into an account. They will then offer you a line of credit equal to the amount of the deposit. This is a **secure credit card**. This is the company's way of protecting itself. By paying the bill regularly, you can prove you are a good risk and may be able to get a non-secure card.

Managing Your Credit Cards

There are some important things to know about credit cards. The more you know and understand the credit process, the better you can manage your debt. It can be very easy to spend more than you can afford.

Missing a Payment—If you miss a payment, you will be charged a late fee. Some cards may also decrease your credit limit. Fees could be as high as $25 to $50 for each month you are late! You also run the risk of damaging your credit history. The company may even close your account. A closed account means you would not be able to use your card, but you would still need to pay off your balance.

Stolen Credit Cards—If your credit card is stolen, it is very important you contact the credit card company immediately. By reporting it to the company as soon as you discover it missing, you can limit the amount you may have to pay if someone else uses your card. Otherwise, you may have to pay the whole amount!

Summary

Being able to manage your money is critical for success in the United States. It is also important to save so you can provide for yourself when you retire. Understanding the value of the currency, setting up banking accounts, and establishing credit are important things to do.

Note: This chapter was written for informative purposes only. We are in no way trying to give any type of legal or financial advice to the reader.

Resources

You can check your credit rating by ordering a copy of your report from each of the three major credit-reporting agencies:

- Equifax
- Trans Union
- Experian.

These companies track your credit history. It is very important you know what is on your file with each of these agencies. Make sure all the information they have is correct.

You can get a copy for under $10 or you may be able to receive a free copy of your credit report. Check with the company to see if you are eligible for a free copy.

Equifax: 1/800/685-1111
Equifax Credit Information Services
P.O. Box 740241
Atlanta, Georgia 30374

Trans Union: 1/800/888-4213
Trans Union Consumer Disclosure
P.O. Box 1000
Chester, PA 19022

Experian: 1/888/397-3742
P.O. Box 9595
Allen, Texas 75013-9595

Glossary

ATM card: a card issued by a bank that, when used with a Personal Identification Number (PIN) of your choosing, allows you to use an automatic teller machine.

Automatic Teller Machine (ATM): a device, usually located on a bank's property, that permits you to perform simple banking transactions without the aid of a human teller.

Cash: another name for currency.

Cashing a check: going to the bank and depositing your check or exchanging your paycheck for currency.

Certificate of deposit (CD): an account where you deposit your money with the bank for a certain length of time, and they pay you a set interest rate.

Check: a paper, used in conjunction with a checking account, that identifies you and your account and authorizes a payee to receive the amount you specify from your account.

Checking account: a bank account from which funds may be drawn by the use of a check.

Credit card: a plastic card issued by a bank to be used instead of cash or a check to purchase items.

Credit rating: a record of how well you pay your bills.

Debit card: a card issued by a bank and used like a credit card that functions as an electronic check.

Dollar: the main unit of U.S. currency.

Interest: the fee paid to borrow money or an amount earned on money deposited..

Interest rate: the percentage the bank will charge you for borrowing money.

Investment account: an account where you give your money to a bank for them to use and they pay you interest on the money in the account.

Loan: credit you receive from a bank, credit union, or loan/lending companies.

Monthly charge account: a credit account where whatever money you charge during the month is due at the end of the month.

Mortgage: a type of loan used for buying a house and having a longer repayment period than many other kinds of loans.

Retirement: the time when people are older and have finished working.

Revolving charge account: a credit account where you need not pay the full amount due, but you are charged interest for any unpaid amount that carries forward to the next month.

Savings account is a bank account in which you keep money for a long period of time.

Volatility: how risky an investment is.

Exercises

1. Internet Exercise (see Pages 211-212 for more information on the Internet): Log on to any search engine (www.google.com, www.dogpile.com, www.yahoo.com) and search by the following terms to learn more about American currency, saving and spending:

    - American currency
    - International exchange rate
    - United States Banking System
    - FDIC
    - Checking and savings accounts
    - Debit cards
    - Secure credit cards
    - Non-secure credit cards
    - American Express
    - Visa
    - MasterCard
    - Revolving credit
    - Loans
    - Mortgages
    - Credit Rating
    - Interest rate.

2. Look up in your local newspaper the exchange rate for the U.S. dollar and your home country's currency. How much of your home country's currency do you get for one U.S. dollar? In America, your local newspaper costs you 25 cents. What would it cost you in your home country?

Chapter 6

Housing

America offers you many choices about where to live. You may choose to live with family or friends when you first arrive in America. After a time, you may want to live on your own. Here we will look at the different options for housing in the United States.

The United States is a large country. You can live anywhere from a big city to a small town. The work you choose may determine where you live. Other factors such as the cost of living, distance to your family, or the climate can help you decide where to live. If you have children, you will need to consider school locations. You may also want to consider the distance to your workplace when choosing where to live. If you are living alone and trying to save money, you may want a roommate, or someone to live with you and share housing expenses. It is a good idea to choose someone you know. You may want to consider someone you work with or know from a group you belong to.

Common Housing Options in the United States

While different housing options are available across the country, most people live in one of the following types of housing:

Apartment - A group of rooms in a building or house. Different people live in the same building. You pay a monthly fee to the owner of the building (landlord) for use of the apartment. The owner maintains the apartment.

House - A building serving as a dwelling for one or more persons, especially for a family. Usually a single home, unconnected to other buildings.

Condominium - An apartment or house you own. Common parts of the property, such as

> **In This Chapter**
> - Types of housing
> - Renting or owning
> - Home/renter's insurance
> - Utilities, services and appliances
> - Moving into your home
> - Basics of renting
> - Buying and owning a home

the grounds and building structure, are owned and maintained jointly by the unit owners.

Trailer/Mobile Home - A prefabricated home put together in sections and can be moved from one area to another. Groups of homes are built or placed together in an area to form a community.

Renting

Many different families live in an apartment building.

Renting an apartment is the most common choice for immigrants. It can take many years to save enough money to buy a home. In some larger cities in the United States, the cost to own a home may be so great that renting is the best choice. When you rent, you pay a monthly fee to the **landlord** for the use of the apartment. The landlord who owns the apartments or rental property can be a person or a company. The owner maintains the apartment and grounds.

You can rent apartments in large buildings with many other people, you can rent rooms in an individual house, or you might rent a whole house. Some people rent out their apartments or houses when they will be gone for a long period of time. There are many different options. Most larger apartments have a **superintendent,** sometimes referred to as the "super." This is the person that maintains or repairs the rental property. Many times the superintendent lives in the apartment complex.

The Fair Housing Act

Federal law prohibits housing discrimination based on your race, color, national origin, religion, sex, family status, or disability. There are a couple of exceptions where someone may choose not to accept you as a tenant:

1) *Mrs. Murphy exception- 4 units or less and the landlord is a resident.*

2) *If you and your roommates are not biologically related (family).*

3) *If the housing code limits how many can stay in a residence. Some immigrants have a pattern of moving in with other families making the total number of people in the specific square footage too many for the size of the space.*

We recommend you check with the local HUD office (U.S. Department of Housing and Urban Development) or visit the website www.hud.gov/ for local and regional housing guidelines and resources. It can be especially helpful when you change from being a renter to wanting to be a homeowner.

Things to Look for When Renting

When looking to rent, the first thing to consider is how much the **rent**, or monthly payment, will be. You may also be required to pay a **security deposit**. This means you have to give one or two months' rent to the apartment owner. This is to cover damage you might do to the apartment. If, when you move out, everything is in good shape, you should get this deposit back. If the landlord or superintendent find damage, they may keep the deposit to repair the damage. Some landlords will automatically keep a portion of the deposit to have the apartment cleaned professionally.

Inspect the Apartment First—It is very important for you to inspect your apartment or rental. Take note of any and all damage that exists in the apartment before you move in. Give a copy of this list to the landlord before you move. You do not want to be held responsible for damage you did not do.

Utilities—Some apartments include utilities. **Utilities** are the services of electricity, natural gas, water, and sewage. Some rental prices may include water or heating or electric. When you are looking at your monthly expenses, you will need to include additional money for utilities. Phone service is not normally included.

Appliances—Many apartments include the basic appliances of a refrigerator/freezer and a stove with an oven. More expensive apartments may contain an automatic dishwasher and/or a washer and dryer. The landlord is responsible for the

---

Helpful Hints When Renting

Consider these guidelines when preparing to rent:

✦ *Have your credit report ready with references*

✦ *Read your lease or agreement carefully, pay attention to exceptions for pets or businesses*

✦ *Get all agreements in writing*

✦ *Be prepared to put down a damage deposit, that should be returned to you provided you leave the rental space in excellent condition when you leave – understand the terms by reading your lease*

✦ *Know your right to privacy*

✦ *Know your rights to have a livable space; weatherproofing; heat, water and electricity; and a clean, sanitary and structurally safe rental*

✦ *Keep communicating with the landlord about repairs and time lines*

✦ *Purchase renter's insurance*

✦ *Get a copy of local laws regarding safety devices such as smoke detectors and deadbolt locks*

✦ *Know when to fight an eviction notice and when to leave – losing a lawsuit can cost hundreds to thousands of dollars.*

maintenance on these appliances. If you have any problems with the equipment, notify the superintendent or landlord.

Services—A benefit of living in an apartment is the apartment owners provide the maintenance and upkeep. For example, if your drain is clogged, you could call your superintendent or building manager to fix it. Many apartments also have a pool and recreational facilities for its tenants' use. They usually provide a laundry room with washers and dryers for your use.

Renter's Insurance

Your personal belongings or the contents of the apartment are not the responsibility of the apartment owner. If you are robbed or if your property is destroyed in a fire, you would have to replace everything yourself. If you are going to rent, it is a good idea to purchase **renter's insurance**. This insures all your property in case of loss or damage, meaning the insurance company would give you money to replace your belongings.

Common Appliances

Refrigerator/Freezer

Dishwasher

Stove/Oven

Clothes Washer

Clothes Dryer

Buying a House

One of the greatest benefits of purchasing a house or a condominium is ownership. When you choose to own, you are paying toward property that should be more valuable in the future. Also, the money you pay toward your loan retains its value. This is called **equity**. A disadvantage of owning a home is you must do all the maintenance and upkeep on your property. You do not need to have the entire purchase price of a house when you choose to buy a house. Most people buy a

Owning a home is a good investment.

house by making a down payment and getting a long-term home loan, or **mortgage**.

Know What You Want

When you start to look for a house, you need to consider how much money you can spend and what kind of house you want. You actually look at many of the same features as in a rental apartment.

What Can You Afford?—Determine how much you can afford to pay a month on a mortgage (house loan), insurance, taxes, and utilities. Consider how much you can spend on a **down payment**, or initial payment, on the house. You may want to consider a pre-approved mortgage, where a bank approves you for a mortgage at a certain amount before you find your house.

What Features Do You Need?—Make a list of the features you need a house to have. How many bedrooms do you need? How many bathrooms do you want? Do you want a house with a garage or a fireplace? Also, decide what style of house you like. Some styles of homes are ranch (a one-story house), colonial (a two-story house), or tri-level (a three-story house). Do you want an older or newer home? Once you have a list, it is time to start looking.

Finding a House to Buy

In most areas, when a house is for sale, there is a "For Sale" sign in the front yard of the house. You can also look in the classified ads of a newspaper or on the Internet. The easiest way to buy a home is to use the services of a realtor. A **realtor** is a person who specializes in helping people find homes. The realtor can help you look for homes and help you understand how to buy a home. They often know the local communities, the quality and safety of the neighborhoods, and can offer advice when purchasing a home. The realtor makes money from the sale of a home, so you do not have to pay any money to the realtor.

A realtor can help find the right house for you.

Selecting a realtor is an important task. There are many realtors in your area. If you do not know where to start looking for a realtor, talk to friends and co-workers. It can be helpful to start with real estate companies in the area. Once you have selected a company, call and make an appointment to meet with a staff member. When you meet with a realtor, show him or her the list you have made of what you need in a house. Tell him or her how much you think you can afford. Tell the realtor where you would like to live, what part of the city, what neighborhoods, etc. They will take note of the items on your list and try to find houses that match your list. A realtor can also help you decide how much you can afford.

Selecting a House

Once the realtor has a list of homes you may like, he or she will make appointments for you to look at houses. If you like a house, but you are not sure if you would like to buy it, you can visit a house several times. Once you think you have found a house you want to buy, you make an offer to the seller. You can negotiate on the selling price of the home. The seller may make a counteroffer, where they agree to sell it to you if you meet their conditions. Then you can accept their offer or make another offer.

Once your offer to buy the house is accepted, you have the right to ask for an inspection of the property. If you request an inspector, you may have to pay for the cost of the inspection. An inspection will let you know if the home needs any repairs.

Have your new house inspected before you buy.

It is very important to have the following items inspected:

- **Pests**—Are there any signs of termites, roaches, or mice?
- **Roof**—How many layers does the roof have? How old is the newest layer? Is the roof damaged?
- **Pipes and drains**—What are the pipes made of? Do the pipes leak? Are the drains clean?
- **Electrical wiring**—How old is the wiring? What kinds of wires were used? How much power can the wiring handle?
- **The structure**—Do the walls, windows, or any brick need to be repaired? Does the house need to be painted? How sturdy is the foundation? If there is a basement, does it leak? Is there any evidence of water damage?

- **Radon, lead, or other chemicals**—Most inspectors can test for dangerous chemicals. It is important to test for lead in older homes.
- **Appliances**—How old are the furnace, dishwasher, refrigerator, water heater, etc.? Do the appliances work?

The Mortgage

Once you have found your house, it is time to finance it! Most people take out a home mortgage loan for a term of 15 or 30 years. There are several things you need to know when financing a house. First, lenders require a down payment from the person buying the house. How much of a down payment depends on the type of mortgage you get. For example, if you get a **conventional mortgage**, you are required to put down 20% of the price of the house. There are also mortgages designed to help first-time buyers. These mortgages allow a lower down payment, but may cost more over the life of the loan. You can get a **pre-approved mortgage.** A pre-approved mortgage is a mortgage you can get before you choose a house, that includes a set amount you can afford. There are many options for mortgaging your home. Your realtor can help you understand the different choices.

Closing on a House

Closing Costs

Once you have found your home and have arranged your mortgage, the realtor will then set an appointment to "close on the house." **Closing** is when you actually buy the house. There are additional costs associated with this process. **Closing costs** are costs you have to pay in order to purchase the house. Make sure you ask your lending institution or realtor how much your closing costs will be. These costs will be your responsibility and they vary depending upon the amount of the mortgage, etc.

Homeowner's Insurance and Taxes

There are two more expenses to consider when purchasing a house: property taxes and home insurance (sometimes referred to as homeowner's insurance). **Property taxes** are the taxes you pay to the government, usually twice a year, for owning the property. If you do not pay your property taxes, the government would have the right to take your home. **Homeowner's insurance** is like renter's insurance, where an insurance company would give you money to replace your belongings and repair or rebuild your house if you had damage to your home. In many states, you must have homeowner's insurance to get a mortgage.

When you close on the house, your lending institution will require proof you have purchased insurance. You will be required to have home insurance as long as you have a mortgage. Some lending institutions set up a special account called an escrow account. An **escrow account** is an account where extra money is deposited from your mortgage payment. This will allow you to pay small amounts toward taxes and insurance every month as part of your mortgage payment. When the property taxes and homeowner's insurance are due, the money is withdrawn from the escrow account to pay for them.

If you buy a home, you should anticipate paying taxes on its value every year. There may be a variety of payment plans available, including automatically paying it as part of your mortgage payment. Real estate, or land you purchase, is also taxable.

Getting Settled in Your New Home

Whether you are moving into a new apartment or a new house, there are many things you must do to set up your home:

- Set up utility services (electricity, natural gas, water)
- Telephone service setup
- Start other optional services (cable TV, newspaper, etc.)
- Rent or purchase appliances
- Postal delivery (change of address)
- Move into your home.

Utilities

Most homes in America are heated with either electricity or natural gas. Some older homes may have oil furnaces. Most homes in the United States need to have electricity. Your home or apartment may use gas, electricity, or a combination of both. It is important to know what kind of energy the appliances need in your apartment or house. You will need to call the local provider to set up an account to have gas and electric supplied to your house. The same process is true for water/sewer. Some providers require a deposit fee if you have not had an account with them before. Some apartments provide certain utilities as a part of the rent payment. The landlord will let you know which utilities you must pay.

Electric Power—Electric power in the United States may be different from what you are used to in your home country. Electric power is standardized in all states across the country. Electric power is set at 110 volts and 60 cycles. Two hundred and twenty volt power is only used for large appliances like stoves, air conditioners, clothes dryers, etc. If you bring any appliances to America, you may need an adaptor to fit U.S. electrical outlets. If you do not use an adaptor, your appliance may be damaged. This can be very dangerous and may cause a fire. Be very careful when using an appliance not purchased in the United States. In some cases, it may be safer and less expensive to buy a new appliance.

Telephone

The telephone system in America can be very confusing. There are many service providers that will compete for your business. There is usually only one local service provider, but there are many choices for long-distance service. Local calls are phone calls that go to nearby areas. Long-distance calls are calls that connect to other countries, states, or are outside your local calling area.

First, call the local phone service provider. This provider will establish phone service in your home. The provider will assign you a telephone number. Next, choose your long-distance provider. You can find more detail on phone service in Chapter 16, *Telephones and Other Technology*.

Other Services

Cable television—Some people choose to subscribe to cable television for a monthly fee. With cable service you can receive additional programs, movies, and channels on your TV. Many areas have access to cable television. Some rural areas, however, do not have cable service. Some cable companies also offer Internet service. For more information, see Chapter 17, *Mass Communications*.

Garbage removal—In large cities, garbage removal is usually provided and paid as a part of your mortgage or rent. In other places, it may be provided by the city and paid through your taxes. If you rent, your landlord may be required to provide for trash removal. If you live in a rural location, you may have to order service from a waste disposal company.

Newspaper delivery—In most places in the country, you can have your newspapers delivered to your home every day. If you would like this service, call one of the local newspaper offices and subscribe. You may also have papers from other areas and countries delivered to you.

Homeowner's Association Dues—If you buy a home in certain areas, you may need to pay homeowner's association dues. Subdivisions, or neighborhoods, may have an association. Usually neighborhoods have associations that require dues. They may also have rules about the appearance of your home and yard, community pools or playgrounds, additional security, or clubhouses. Your realtor should make you aware of any association before you buy a house or condominium. The dues can go toward the cost of lawn maintenance, snow removal, garbage removal, and upkeep on common property.

Appliances

Most apartments include a refrigerator/freezer and a stove/oven. If you are buying a home, you may need to consider buying appliances. Common large appliances you may find in American homes include: a refrigerator, furnace, water heater, dishwasher, microwave, clothes washer, and clothes dryer.

Some homeowners will sell their appliances with the house. You might want to negotiate the price of appliances into the cost of the home. If you need to purchase appliances, compare prices at different stores. Appliances offered in a department store may vary a great deal in price compared with those sold in a store that only sells appliances. Another way to buy an appliance is through rent-to-own programs. The benefit of these programs is you can pay a monthly fee for the use of the appliance. At the end of a specific time, you will own the appliance. This type of program may cost you more over time than if you had bought the appliance.

Getting Your Mail

Before you move, you should begin to tell people your new address. Go to the local post office and fill out a change-of-address form. This will make sure your mail will be sent to your new address. You can change your address with creditors when you pay your bills. Most magazines list a phone number for changing subscriptions. The post office will forward your first-class mail to your new address for one year. Magazines and newspapers will be forwarded for 60 days. Be sure you have notified everyone by this time.

The U.S. Postal Service—Your local post office offers a variety of important services. You can locate your local post office through the phone book, or if you have access to a computer, you can go to the post office's website (www.usps.com). At the post office you can:

- Mail envelopes and packages in and out of the country. The most common rate for postage is first-class which is currently 37 cents per first ounce.
- Buy postage stamps. You can also buy postage stamps in many grocery stores.
- Complete a change-of-address form. If you move, this form will insure your mail is forwarded to you.
- Rent a post office box, located at the post office, also known as a P.O. Box for a fee per year. This is a good option if you are moving frequently and do not want to keep changing your address.

The post office will return mail if you do not use the right amount of postage.

Properly address your letters:

- Stamps go on the upper right corner of the envelope.
- If you do not put enough postage on an envelope or package, it will be returned to you.

Moving In

Whether you are moving into an apartment or a house, you will need to arrange to move your belongings. You may ask friends and family to help you move. You might rent a van or truck to help transport your belongings. You can choose to hire a **moving company**. A moving company is paid to move your belongings. Some may pack your clothes and personal items for additional fees. They may charge additional fees for boxes in which to pack your belongings. The boxes are moved with your furniture.

Summary

This chapter is intended to help you understand some of what you will encounter when looking for housing. It is not meant to be all-inclusive or to recommend any services or approaches to home buying or renting.

When renting or buying, your credit and budget are important. When buying a house, you may need to have a realtor, inspection, and a lending institution. It is important to decide how much you can afford to spend on a home. There are many services and resources to help you buy a home. Buying a home will cost you more than the price of the house. Closing costs, moving costs, utility deposits, and inspection fees are some of the additional expenses involved in buying a home.

Glossary

Closing: is when you actually buy the house.

Closing costs: costs you pay in order to purchase a house, including down payments, escrow, commissions, and taxes.

Conventional mortgage: requires you to put down 20% of the price of the house.

Down payment: the initial payment on a house.

Equity: the money you pay toward your loan.

Escrow account: an account where extra money is deposited from your mortgage payment, allowing you to pay small amounts toward taxes and insurance every month as part of your mortgage payment.

Homeowner's insurance: coverage against specific loss on your house in return for paying premiums.

Landlord: the person or company who owns the apartments or rental property.

Mortgage: a long-term home loan. A fixed interest rate mortgage will have the same interest rate for the whole length of the mortgage. A variable interest rate mortgage will have an interest rate that changes, based on the current national interest rate.

Moving company: a company hired to move your belongings.

Pre-approved mortgage: a mortgage you can get before you choose a house. It is set to an amount you can afford.

Property taxes: the taxes you pay the government, usually twice a year, for owning a property.

Realtor: a person who specializes in helping people find homes.

Rent: monthly payment for housing.

Renter's insurance: insures all your property in case of loss or damage, meaning the insurance company would give you money to replace your belongings.

Security deposit: an amount of money, usually the value of one or two months' rent, required by apartment complexes to cover damage you might do to the apartment.

Superintendent: the person who maintains or repairs the rental property.

Utilities: the services of electricity, natural gas, water, and sewage.

Exercises

1. Internet Exercise (see Pages 209-210 for more information on the Internet): Log on to any search engine (www.google.com, www.dogpile.com, www.yahoo.com) and search by the following terms to learn more about housing in America:

   - Housing options
   - Rentals
   - Apartment guide
   - Varieties of homes
   - What to look for when renting
   - Home inspections
   - Renter's insurance
   - First time home buyer
   - Closing costs on a home
   - Homeowner's taxes
   - Homeowner's insurance
   - Moving
   - Utilities

2. Pick up a rental magazine or your local newspaper that has a rental section. Choose three properties you may be interested in. Start with $750 a month to pay for all the costs involved with renting a home (including things like deposit, gas, electric, phone, parking, etc . . .). Can you afford the property you want? What things can you do to make the property more affordable? This will take a little bit of research, but will be helpful when you are ready to get out on your own.

Chapter 7

Transportation

Getting Around in the United States

Understanding and using the different transportation options available will help you to be more independent.

Most large cities have some type of public transportation. Types of public transportation include buses, taxis, trains, and subway systems.

The United States does not have a passenger train system in every part of the country. Many rural areas do not have public transportation options at all. In these areas, you may want to use a car for transportation.

Getting from state to state, or from city to city, can be done in many ways. There are buses and trains that travel across America. You can purchase tickets to travel on buses or trains at their stations. The most popular way to travel around the country is by plane or by automobile (car). Airfare for planes can be expensive, however it is the quickest and easiest way to travel. You will learn much more about cars later in this chapter.

Local Transportation

If you work or live in a large city, you will have some type of public transportation available. Buses, trains, taxis, and subways can move you throughout a city.

Buses

A city bus is an inexpensive method of traveling around town. Larger cities usually have a bus, or metro system. Each bus has a specific route it takes through the city. Not all

In This Chapter
- Using a bus
- Using a subway
- Using a taxi
- Getting a driver's license
- The Bureau of Motor Vehicles
- Buying a car
- Driving a car

buses go to all areas of the city. You may need to transfer among several buses to get to your destination. Look for a map of the bus system showing all the routes, the riding information, and the exact locations where the bus stops. Depending on your location, buses may run 24 hours a day or they may only run during daytime hours.

Most cities have a bus system.

Most bus systems accept cash, tokens, or a transportation card for payment. Tokens and cards are usually purchased at bus stations or from machines near bus stops. When cash is used, be prepared to have **exact change** (or the precise amount of money needed to purchase your fare).

How to Ride the Bus—Bus stops are usually located at or around street corners. A sign marks every bus stop, and sosme stops will even have shelters. Most bus stops also include a route map and bus schedule. Before you get on the bus, be sure to read the **destination sign** on the front of the bus. The destination sign tells you where the bus is going.

Most buses stop about every two or three blocks. Many buses have a tape strip located above or between the windows. Push this strip to signal the driver to stop.

When you get on the bus, there will be a **fare box**. The fare box is where you put your money or tokens to pay for the ride. You may need to transfer from one bus to another. You can usually get a transfer, for no charge, as long as you use it within a short period of time. You can request a transfer pass from the driver of the bus you are on. When you get on the new bus, give the transfer pass to the driver of the new bus.

Riding the city bus can be confusing the first few times you use the system. It is always a good idea to have a friend or mentor show you how the bus system works. Bus companies have maps and schedules that will help you find your way. Communities will often print bus routes in the local phone book as well.

Commuter Trains and the Subway

Commuter trains and subway systems are found in many larger cities. Many people live outside the city, in the suburbs, and commute into the city to work each day by train. Commuter trains usually run between suburban areas and the center of the city. There may be a limited number of stops on a commuter train. Schedules are available at the commuter train station.

A subway is another type of train system. Subways only operate in large cities. They make more frequent stops than commuter trains. Some subways operate above ground, and others operate only underground. Subway systems work like buses. You may need to transfer between trains to get to your destination. Schedules and tokens are available at the subway station.

How to Ride the Subway—When you go to the subway station, you will see booths and turnstiles. Agents (people working in the booth) can give you directions, subway maps, and tokens or cards to pay for fares. You will pay your fare before you go through the turnstile by either inserting tokens into the turnstile or sliding your card through the slot in the turnstile.

- After you go through the turnstile, you will see signs that will direct you to the correct train platform (train stop).
- At the platform there will be signs that indicate which trains stop there and where the trains are going. In many instances, several trains will stop at the same platform. Check the front or side of the train for the route number or letter. The route number or letter indicates where the train will be going. Be sure to board the correct train and do not be afraid to ask agents for help.
- Before you board the train, wait until the people who want to get off have left the train.
- As you board the train, be careful of the gap between the platform and the train.
- As the train is moving, conductors (train drivers) make stop announcements. Pay attention to the announcements so you do not miss your stop.
- To be sure you are traveling in the right direction, check the subway map.

The subway system can be very confusing. Take your mentor or a friend on your first subway trip.

Taxi Service

A **taxicab** is a car you can hire to take you from one place to another. In larger cities, taxicabs are a common way for people to get around town. They charge a small initial fee and add charges for each mile or minute you travel. Taxis can be expensive if you are going a long distance.

You can get a taxi in a few ways. Ways to get a taxicab include:

- At a taxi stand found at hotels and airports
- Calling a taxicab company and giving them the address of where you are

- Hailing a taxi.

You can hail, or signal, for a taxi whenever you see one on the street. To hail a taxi, simply raise or wave your hand at them. You know the taxi is available if the light on the roof of the taxi is on. If the light is off, the taxi is occupied.

You will need to tell the driver of the taxi the address you want to go to. Do not give your destination before you enter the cab. Wait until you are inside. Most people give the driver a tip of 10 to 15% of the total bill. If you are in a smaller city or town, you will probably need to phone the taxi company to have a car sent to your address.

Driving a Car in the United States

If you do not live in a large city, or if you live outside the bus area, you will probably need to use a car to get from place to place. Driving a car is the most common form of transportation in America.

Getting a Driver's License

To drive a car in the United States, you need to have a valid driver's license issued by the motor vehicle department of the state you live in. An international driver's license is not required in the United State as long as you have an American license. You can drive in America with a valid driver's license from your home country and an international driver's license until you get your American driver's license.

If you do not have a driver's license, you can get one from the motor vehicle department in your local area. Each state has different rules and regulations for getting a driver's license. Be sure to learn your state's automotive rules and regulations. Laws vary by state. You will need to renew your driver's license every few years. Some states offer their driver's tests in languages other than English.

Motor Vehicles Department—If you plan to own and operate a car, then you will need to visit the motor vehicle department. The **Motor Vehicle Department** is a governmental office run by each individual state. The motor vehicle department can have different names in each state. Common names of the motor vehicle department include:

- Bureau of Motor Vehicles (BMV)
- Department of Motor Vehicles (DMV)
- Registry of Motor Vehicles (RMV).

The motor vehicle department makes sure everyone who owns a vehicle has the appropriate insurance and licenses. The most common reason people go to this office is to get a driver's license. People also renew license plates there for their cars once a year.

Photo ID—Even if you are not planning to drive a vehicle, you will want to go to the motor vehicle department to get a photo ID. You will need a photo ID to:

- Cash or write checks
- Open bank accounts
- Fly on airlines
- Perform other activities.

Motor vehicle departments are typically very busy at the beginning and end of each month.

Learning Permit—Before you can practice driving or take driving lessons, you need a learner's permit. A **learner's permit** allows you to drive a car as long as there is another licensed driver with you. In order to get your learner's permit, you should go to your local motor vehicle department. Be prepared to show your proof of name and proof of age. Showing them your valid visa or passport can do this.

Taking Driving Lessons—If you want to learn how to drive a car, you may want to consider taking driving lessons from a driving school. In order to take driving lessons, you must first get a learner's permit. There are many places you can take classes to learn to drive. A spouse, friend, or family member who has a driver's license can teach you how to drive. Many high schools offer driver's training. There are also many driving schools where you can go and pay to learn how to drive.

> **Getting a Driver's License**
>
> - Get a permit to drive from the BMV
> - Practice driving with another driver or go to a driving school
> - Study the driving rules
> - Go to the BMV to take a written test and eye exam and a driving test
> - If you pass all tests, you receive a driver's license
> - You may need to renew your license after several years.

The Driving Test—Once you have completed your driving lessons and feel you are ready to drive, you will need to take a driving test. To take a driving test, you need to return to the motor vehicle department. There you will take two tests:

- Written (the rules of driving)

✦ Driving (your skill at driving the car).

You can get an information booklet from the motor vehicle department to help you prepare for the written exam. The driving test will be done with an agent of the motor vehicle department. You will need to pass both tests to receive a driver's license. There is a small fee for your driver's license.

Immigrant Views

"The day I passed my driver's test, I became independent to move around. Before obtaining my license, I had to have my brother take me to find a job and drop me off at work."

Jairam Kahon immigrated from Batala, India in 1989.

Owning a Car

Whether you are commuting to work or going across the country, a car is the most common mode of transportation in America. Many Americans consider a car to be a necessity. If you live in a rural area, public transportation may be unavailable. If you live in a large city, some attractions, such as shopping centers, may be difficult to get to without a car.

Buying a Car

If you want to own a car, you have a couple of different options. You can buy a new car from a car dealership, buy a used car someone else has driven, or lease a car. Your decision to buy a car or lease a car will depend on how much money you have (or want to spend), how long you will need the car, and what kind of car you want to drive. New cars can be very expensive. Many people purchase a used car for their first vehicle. Some people sell their own used cars. You may be able to find a good vehicle for a lower price from an individual.

Many people buy used cars.

Before you buy, be sure to compare prices, test drive the car and have it checked by a mechanic if possible. Buy your car from a person or business with a good reputation. When leasing a car, you basically rent the car for several years, then return it at the end of the agreement. You are responsible for the condition of the car.

Compare Prices—Compare the prices of different types of cars and at different car dealerships (places that sell cars). Prices may be different at each dealership. Research the different types of cars and buying options. You can go to your local library to find reference books that list the make, model, and year of each type car and its current value. The Internet is also a great place to research and compare cars.

Take a Test Drive—When you have found a car you like, you should take it for a **test drive**. The dealer will ride with you as you drive the car. You can decide if the car is right for you. You can negotiate with the salesperson on the price of the car.

Financing the Car

Cars are expensive. Most people in America buy a car with an auto loan. **Auto loans** allow you to pay for a car in monthly installments. Auto loans also allow you to pay for the car over a period of time, usually between two and six years. Dealerships can assist you with your auto loan, or financing, at the dealership. You can apply for an auto loan on your own from your local bank. You will need to have of the information about the car and selling price in order to do this.

Car dealers can help you get financing for your car.

Automobile Insurance

Auto insurance is required in almost every state. **Auto insurance** protects you against financial losses if your car is damaged or if you damage someone else's car. Some insurance will even help you if your car is stolen. Most states require you to have proof of insurance before you can purchase a vehicle. The cost of your insurance will vary depending on the type of vehicle you buy. Often, the most popular cars or cars with a good safety record will cost less to insure. Older used cars will cost less to insure. Find an insurance company before you buy a car. An insurance agent can help you understand how much car insurance will cost.

When you buy insurance, you receive an insurance **policy**. The policy is a written description of what you are insured for. Keep your insurance policy for your records. Most insurance companies also issue a card with your name and policy information on it. It is a good idea to keep this card with you, or in the vehicle, at all times.

Most insurance companies have you pay for the policy on a regular basis. When you make your payment, you are paying **premiums**. A premium is just another way of saying "paying in installments."

If you have an accident or your car is vandalized or stolen, you can file a **claim** with the insurance company. A claim is a formal request for the insurance company to pay for any damages done to your car, or any other cars damaged in the accident. A claim is also a formal request to pay for any medical bills you, or others, may have because of an accident.

When you file a claim, an insurance agent from the insurance company may come and look at your car or you may be asked to go to a claim center or a repair shop to have the car inspected. If the damages are covered by your policy, your claim will be accepted (your insurance will pay for the repairs to the car). If you caused the accident, however, the insurance company will also pay to repair the other person's vehicle and any medical costs for the injured person.

> **If your car is damaged or in an accident**
>
> You should:
>
> ✦ Not leave the scene of an accident
>
> ✦ Call the police and report the incident
>
> ✦ Obtain insurance and registration information from the other people involved in the accident
>
> ✦ Obtain a copy of the police report for your records and for the insurance company.

There are many kinds of auto insurance. Not all insurance policies protect you in the same way. Be sure your insurance agent fully explains the kinds of insurance available. Be sure you understand the type of coverage you will be paying for.

License Plates

You need to go to your local motor vehicle department to buy license plates for your car. You will need to bring proof of insurance and proof you have purchased the car. Your car will be registered (listed as legal) under your name. You should expect to pay a fee and taxes for registering your car.

License plates must be renewed every year.

The motor vehicle department will issue you a license plate to display on the back of your car. Some states also have a plate on the front of the car as well. This plate proves you have registered the vehicle with the state and paid taxes for the vehicle. Every year, you will need to renew your license plates before the expiration date listed on the plate.

Emissions Testing

In some states you may need to take your car for emissions testing. An **emissions test** is done to make sure your car does not produce too much pollution. There will be a variety of emissions testing sites in your community. If your car passes the emissions test, you will receive a pass document and a sticker. Display the sticker on your car. Take the pass document to the motor vehicle department when you go to renew your license plates.

If your car fails emissions testing, you would need to repair your car. Once the repairs are complete, have the car retested. In states that require emissions testing, you cannot get license plates without passing emissions testing. New cars are tested by the dealership.

Caring for Your Car

It is important to maintain your car. By getting the proper maintenance for your car, you will keep your car safe to drive. Maintenance will also help prevent damage to your car. For normal maintenance on your car, you can use:

- Service stations—service station is a fuel station that also repairs cars
- A full service repair shop
- Specialty shops—specialty shop may only work on certain parts of a car or perform certain kinds of maintenance, such as an oil change, exhaust repair, brake replacement, or tire replacement
- Car dealerships.

You can find automotive repair shops listed in the phone directory.

Driving on the Road

It is helpful to understand how U.S. roadways are organized. There are several types of roadways including:

- Interstates
- Expressways

- State roads
- County roads
- Town and city streets
- Toll roads, toll bridges, and toll tunnels.

Interstates are roads that cross state borders. Many interstates are also expressways. **Expressways** are roads that may have many lanes for traffic. Expressways do not have stoplights or stop signs. Expressways may have a higher speed limit than some other types of roads. Some expressways have a minimum speed you must maintain.

State and **county** roads are roads that stay in the state or county. They may have stoplights or stop signs. Sometimes, state or county roads are called local roads.

Town and **city** streets are the local roadways around cities. These streets are usually numbered or named. They have many stop signs and streetlights you will need to be aware of. Some of the streets only allow you to travel in one direction (one-way streets). You must pay close attention to signs and lights when driving in the city. You can obtain local maps from gas stations, convenience stores, bookstores, and libraries.

Finally, there are roads you have to pay a fee to drive on. **Toll roads** require you to pay a fee after you have traveled a certain number of miles and before you exit the road. There are also places in the country that have **toll bridges** or **toll tunnels**. There are some bridges and tunnels you have to pay to cross over or go through. Not all bridges and tunnels in America charge a toll. The tolls for roads, bridges, and tunnels help to pay for maintenance that keeps the routes safe for use. Most road maps of the United States can help you see what kinds of roads you may be traveling on.

Lanes and Exits

Driving on expressways, or highways, can be confusing. Expressways, or highways, have several lanes. The left lanes are used for passing slower traffic. Travelers that drive at the maximum speed limit and will not be leaving the expressway for a long period of time use the center lanes. Right lanes are used for local traffic that will be exiting or entering the expressway.

In some parts of the country, there are special lanes used for different types of driving:

- The **express** lane is a lane you should use if you do not need to exit the road for a long distance. Traffic on express lanes usually travels more quickly because people are not slowing down to exit or enter.
- **HOV** (Highly Occupied Vehicle), or carpool lanes, are sometimes found in areas that have high traffic. They are to be used only by cars that have more than two or three people in the car. HOV lanes encourage people to share rides.
- **Service roads** are roads alongside the expressway. They may be used to exit and enter the expressway.
- **Exits** are the ramps that allow you to leave the expressway.

A Word from Kooner...

Plan a short trip around town. Find the local grocery store, bank, the motor vehicle department, the local library, the local airport, etc. My nephew did this all by himself! He got lost, but he did not panic. He stopped and asked for directions, practiced his local driving, and made sure he came back before dark! Once you get familiar with the driving laws and the area, practice your highway driving!

Summary

Learning to use public transportation or how to drive can help you become very independent quickly. Take time to research the transportation options your city or state provides. Transportation is an important part of the American society.

A car will help you to go where you want, when you want. Take the time to get a car that is best for you. Learn the local rules and regulations for driving. Get familiar with your area, and enjoy your independence!

Glossary

Auto loans: allow you to pay for a car in monthly installments.

Destination sign: a sign on the front of a bus telling you where the bus is going.

Emissions test: a test, required in some states, to make sure your car does not produce too much pollution.

Exact change: the precise amount of money needed to purchase your fare.

Exits: the ramps that allow you to leave an expressway.

Express lane: a lane for vehicles that do not need to exit the road for a long distance.

Expressways: roads that have many lanes for traffic.

Fare box: where you put your money or tokens to pay for a bus ride.

HOV (Highly Occupied Vehicle) lane: lane set aside for vehicles containing more than two or three people. Sometimes called "carpool lanes."

Insurance: a contract with a company to protect you against financial losses if your car is damaged or if you damage someone else's car.

Insurance claim: a formal request for the insurance company to pay for any damages done to your car, or any other cars damaged in an accident.

Insurance policy: a written description of the risks you are insured against and the amounts you and the insurance company agree to pay if an accident occurs.

Insurance premium: the amount of money you pay to the insurance company on a regular basis to keep the insurance coverage active.

Interstate highways: roads that cross state borders. Many interstates are also expressways.

Learner's permit: allows you to drive a car as long as there is another licensed driver with you.

Motor Vehicle Department: is a governmental office run by each individual state.

Service roads: roads beside an expressway that may be used to exit and enter the expressway.

Taxicab: a car you can hire to take you from one place to another.

Test drive: an opportunity to drive a car before purchasing it, to check it for any problems and decide if you like the car.

Toll roads: roads that require you to pay a fee after you have traveled a certain number of miles and before you exit the road. Toll bridges and toll tunnels require you to pay to cross over or go through.

Exercises

1. Internet Exercise (see Pages 211-212 for more information on the Internet): Log on to any search engine (www.google.com, www.dogpile.com, www.yahoo.com) and search by the following terms to learn more about

transportation. For many of these, you may choose to put the name of the city or state you live in before the word or phrase. Doing this will bring up local information as well as national information.

- Transportation
- Department of Transportation
- Riding the bus
- How to ride the subway system
- American railways
- Getting a taxi(cab)
- Driver's license
- Department of Motor Vehicles
- Driving lessons
- How to buy a car
- Automobile financing
- Automobile insurance
- Emissions testing
- Road maps and atlas
- Driving in America.

2. Pick up a local bus, train, or subway schedule. Choose a destination you would like to visit. Sit with a friend and plan the trip. You will need to be sure to estimate the amount of time you will need to get to and from the destination, as well as the costs you will have to be prepared for. Once you have the trip planned, you might even have an adventure!

CHAPTER 8

SHOPPING

So Many Choices...

Shopping in the United States can be an adventure. Spend a few minutes in a grocery store and look at the many choices available. You can buy fruits and vegetables from around the world at any time of the year. Americans value variety and convenience. Americans also like to save time. These values are reflected in the way we shop and the products we buy.

Why are there so many choices? Anyone in America can sell services or goods. **Consumers** are the people who buy goods and services. America is a country of consumers. Consumers let companies know what types of products they need and like by deciding which products to use. Companies use advertising to tell consumers about their products and services.

Where to Shop

Most American lifestyles are fast-paced, focused on time, and looking for convenience. There are many places to shop in the United States.

Supermarkets/Grocery Stores

Large, self-service stores that sell food and household products.

Things you can buy—Food items – fresh produce, frozen foods, canned foods, meat, poultry, ready-to-eat foods, packaged products, cold foods, household goods, cleaners, plastic and paper items, health and beauty products.

> **IN THIS CHAPTER**
> - American shopping
> - Types of stores America has to offer
> - Where to get what you need
> - How to shop in America
> - Clothes shopping

Features—Supermarkets come in many sizes. Some supermarkets are small and locally owned. Others are larger stores run by a major company. Many of the larger stores have several stores across a region of the country. Both the smaller and larger stores provide a supply of fresh, packaged, and frozen foods.

The larger supermarkets:

Local markets can be a good source of fresh produce.

+ Usually have more selection and lower prices than the smaller stores
+ May include pharmacies to sell prescription drugs
+ May be open 24 hours a day for shopping at any time of the day or night.

Department Stores

Stores that sell a wide variety of non-food items and services and are organized in separate departments.

Things you can buy—Clothing for the whole family, shoes, household furnishings, furniture, jewelry, cosmetics, luggage and more.

Features—There are different department stores for different price ranges, high-end, medium, and low-end. High-end stores sell high quality merchandise at a higher price. Low-end stores sell lower quality goods at a lower price.

Superstores

Department stores sell a wide variety of goods.

A combination of a grocery store and department store (Big K, Wal-Mart Super Center, Super Target) or a very large store that includes certain areas such as:

+ Hardware
+ Housewares
+ Garden
+ Sporting goods
+ Toys
+ Cameras and electronics.

Things you can buy—Everything you can buy in a grocery store or mid- to low-priced department store.

Features—

- Large selection of merchandise in one store
- Designed for one-stop shopping (get everything you need in one store)
- Usually have lower prices than smaller stores
- Usually located in the suburbs of a city.

Discount Stores

Stores that sell products at a lower price.

Things you can buy—Unsold merchandise from other department stores or items with reduced prices.

Features—

- The products they sell will change often
- The number of products available will change often
- You can find some very good buys
- Quality of goods may be high or low.

Convenience Stores

Small stores usually attached to a gas station.

Things you can buy—Snacks, drinks, travel supplies, basic groceries, ready-to-eat food, basic auto supplies, milk, bread, cigarettes, soda.

Features—

- Located in local neighborhoods and cities
- Smaller selection of items
- Usually more expensive than grocery stores
- Convenient for quick service.

Drugstore/Pharmacy

Smaller store featuring a pharmacy for buying prescription drugs and over-the-counter health and beauty aids.

Things you can buy—Prescription drugs, medical products, hygiene and beauty supplies, basic grocery items, snacks, soft drinks.

Features—

- Often open 24 hours
- Same features as a convenience store.

Wholesale Clubs

Members-only club – Large warehouses featuring bulk (large-sized) quantities of products at a discounted price (Sam's Club, Costco).

Things you can buy—Large quantity foods, household goods, office supplies, automotive, home goods.

Features—

- You must be a member to shop there
- Low membership fee to join
- Products are geared to business and restaurant use
- Bulk (larger-sized) products are available
- Limited selection of items
- Large quantity of items available
- Prices can be very low.

Specialty Stores

Stores that specialize in a particular product.

Things you can buy—Depends on the type of store:

Go to a:	In order to get:
Dry cleaners	Your laundry cleaned
Florist	Flowers
Hardware store	Tools/lumber
Garden shops	Landscaping products
Clothing stores	Special size/brand name clothing

Go to a:	In order to get:
Sporting goods store	Sporting/outdoor activity products
Automotive	Automobile parts
Office supply stores	Office supplies/computers
Pet stores	Pets and pet supplies
Antique stores	Antiques

Features—

- Offer specific services and products
- May be of better quality
- May offer a larger selection of a specific product.

Shopping Mall

Many specialty stores and department stores can be found in one location.

Things you can buy—Almost anything.

Features—

- Most malls are big buildings with many stores under one roof
- Usually located in the suburban area of a city
- Offers large parking areas
- Convenient to do all your shopping at one place
- Many of the same stores are located in malls across the country.

Shopping malls let you visit many different stores in one location.

Strip Mall

Small groups of specialty stores in a row.

Things you can buy—Depends on the stores.

Features—

- A small, exterior mall
- Each store has its own outside entrance.

Outlet Malls/Factory Outlets

Large outdoor malls selling merchandise at a discounted price.

Things you can buy—Clothing, housewares, specialty items.

Features—

- Major stores selling overstocked merchandise
- Usually lower costs, sometimes lower in quality
- Last season's products
- Usually located outside large cities.

Farmer's Market

Small groups of farmers who sell fresh produce.

Things you can buy—Seasonal fruits and vegetables, freshly canned goods, freshly made bakery goods.

Features—

- Fresh foods
- Products are locally grown and produced
- Good prices.

Farmer's markets offer fresh produce and homemade goods.

Garage Sale/Yard Sale

Individuals or neighborhoods that have an informal sale in their garage or yard.

Things you can buy—Clothing, baby items, housewares, toys, home appliances, furniture, miscellaneous items.

Features—

- Yard sales are a great way to find bargains! People are getting rid of what they no longer need, and they are selling them at low prices.

- Many neighborhoods have a sale weekend, where many people put out their sale items.
- Many items are in good condition. Some things are junk (no good).
- Usually held on Fridays and Saturdays from 8 a.m. to 4 p.m.
- Expect to pay cash for your purchases. Some people may accept checks.
- You can negotiate prices. If you want to pay a lower price, make an offer.
- Be ready to take your purchases with you.

Flea Market

A big yard sale in a specific location, where individual people set up an area and sell their items.

Things you can buy—Clothing, baby items, housewares, toys, home appliances, furniture, miscellaneous stuff.

Features—

- Usually held in a specific location on weekends
- A great place to find bargains
- It is like going to many garage sales in one location
- You may negotiate prices.

Shopping Basics

Here are some suggestions when shopping in the United States:

Understand the Value of Your Money

Learning to work with a different currency can be challenging. You need to understand what money is worth and what your money can buy. The American dollar is worth a certain amount when exchanged for currency from your country. Understanding the **exchange rate** will help you to understand the cost of different products. The exchange rate is

Understand the value of your money.

the cost or benefit of exchanging the currency of your country for American money. The exchange rate may change daily. The Internet has many sites that can assist you with exchange rates.

A Word from Kooner... My nephew had just gotten his first paycheck from his part-time job - $120. He was caught driving too fast by the police and had to pay an $80 ticket. He suddenly realized the value of his money. He worked very hard to earn that $80, and because he chose to break the speed limit, he could not spend his hard-earned money as he pleased. He doesn't speed anymore!

Where You Shop Will Affect the Price You Pay

As discussed earlier, where you choose to shop (what type of store you shop at) will affect the price you pay. You can buy a gallon of milk at a supermarket and a gallon of milk at a convenience store, and you will pay a different price at each store.

Pay the Price Listed—Do Not Barter

Stores sell items for the price listed on the product or on the shelf below the product. Bartering or bargaining on the posted price is not customary in America. Store employees are not allowed to change the price of an item. A company sets the price of an item, and the posted price is the price you will pay. People in the United States only barter when making major purchases, such as a car or home.

Sales Tax

Most states, and some cities, collect a sales tax on items you buy in their area. State taxes usually average 4% to 10% of the total purchase price. For example, in a state with a 5% sales tax, if you buy an item that costs $1 you will pay $1.05 for that item. Some states do not tax clothing purchases, and most states do not tax food, except for food you purchase at a restaurant.

Comparison Shopping

It is helpful to learn how to compare prices. It can be confusing to know which product you should choose with so many products available. Sometimes you will find a better value if you buy a larger size package.

Learn to compare products to find the best value.

Some grocery stores list a unit price on the product or on the shelf under the product. The **unit price** is the price of the product based on the weight or quantity purchased.

Brand-Name Products

Companies spend a lot of time and money to promote their products. **National brands** are products sold throughout America. Large companies usually sell national brands. Most of the advertisements you see on TV, hear on the radio, and read in newspapers and magazines are for national brands.

Store brands or generic brands are products similar to the national brand products. Local supermarket chains package store brands. Store brands and generic brands often cost much less than a national brand.

Sales

Stores often have sales on merchandise. During a sale, some items are sold at a lower price than usual. Stores may have seasonal sales to sell older items or items that are out of season more quickly. Stores may choose to put items on sale to help clear merchandise off the shelves in order to make room for items for the next season. You may want to wait to purchase an item until it goes "on sale." Be careful though, if you wait for a sale, the item may no longer be available.

Typical sales during the year may include:
- February, March, and April – end of winter sales
- May – Mother's Day sales
- June – Father's Day sales
- July, August – end of summer sales
- August, September – back to school sales
- November, December – Holiday sales.

Many stores place sale advertisements in the Sunday newspaper. The sale prices are usually available for the week that follows.

Bar Coding and Pricing

Most products in the American marketplace have a bar code. A **bar code** is a code of lines and number that appears on a product. Store registers can read bar codes quickly and easily. This scanning can help make paying for your purchase faster and easier. The price of the

Most products have bar codes to make purchasing easier.

item may not be printed on the product. You may need to look for the price of the product on the shelf below the product.

Coupons

Companies issue coupons for their products to encourage people to buy them. A **coupon** is an ad that gives you a small discount on a certain product. Coupons are often issued to help promote name-brand products. With a coupon, a national brand may cost less than a store brand. Some stores may have special weeks where they increase the value of your coupons. Coupons may have an expiration date. You must use the coupon before the expiration date to get the discount. There are many different kinds of coupons you can use to save money.

Save Your Receipts

When purchasing goods or services, save your receipts. A receipt serves as proof of purchase. Appliances or electronic equipment, for example, are often under a manufacturer's warranty for a period of time. A **warranty** is a guarantee by the company to repair or replace defective items for a certain period of time after purchase. Many items come with a warranty card you must fill out and return to the manufacturer. You may need to be registered with the company to have an item fixed or replaced.

Receipts are also helpful if you need to return or exchange a purchase. Each store may have its own policy for returning items.

If you buy an item and it goes on sale within a few weeks, some stores give you a price adjustment if you have your receipt. They will give you the difference between the sale price and what you paid for the item.

Tipping for Services

Another common practice in America is tipping. **Tipping** means giving someone an additional amount of money, called a tip or gratuity, for service they have provided or for doing an exceptional job. The amount of a tip can vary from place to place and from service to service. For example, you are expected to tip wait staff in a restaurant from 15% to 20% of the total bill. For other services, a tip may be anywhere from $1 to $5 as the norm. Examples of service providers who would be tipped would include:

- Restaurant waiters and waitresses
- Housekeepers in hotels

- Door/bell persons at hotels
- Taxicab drivers
- Delivery people (like pizza delivery)
- Hair stylists
- Manicurists/pedicurists
- Masseuses/masseurs
- Skycaps at airports.

Catalogs

Many people buy items from store catalogs. Catalogs contain a picture and a description of each item being sold. You can place an order by phone, fax, mail and sometimes the Internet. If you are paying for your merchandise over the telephone, you must use a credit card. If you do not want to use a credit card, you have to fill out a catalog order form. Send the order form with a check for the amount of the item, plus any sales tax and shipping and handling charges, to the company through the mail. Once the company receives your order with payment, they will ship your order to you.

Catalog shopping can save time.

Shopping for Clothes

It is important to try on clothing before you purchase. Clothing stores and department stores have rooms for you to try on clothes. There are separate dressing rooms for men and women. You may need to ask a clerk to let you into the dressing room.

In the United States, men's clothing and women's clothing are sold using different size charts. This is also true of shoes. The size chart for men's feet is different from the chart used to size women's feet. Generally, men's clothing is sold by the measurement of the clothes. In the United States, the basic unit of measurement of length is the inch.

U.S. Customary System: Length

U.S. Unit	Metric Equivalent
1 inch	2.54 centimeters
1 foot (12 inches)	0.3048 meter
1 yard (3 feet)	0.9144 meter

The sizes of men's clothing are often described in inches. For example, a man whose waist is 38 inches around and whose inseam (the length of the inside of the leg) is 40 inches would look for pants that are labeled 38 x 40.

Women's clothing is described in numbered sizes. Clothing manufacturers assign the sizes. Each manufacturer may use different measurements for the same size. Shirts labeled "size 10" by one brand may fit differently from a "size 10" shirt from a different brand. The sizing charts used in the United States may be different from the sizing charts used in your home country. The following sizing charts can help you compare American sizes to sizes from the United Kingdom and Europe.

Clothing Size Chart

Women's Clothing

Juniors 3, 5, 7, 9, 11, 13, 15 – Geared to teen-agers and young women

Misses 2, 4, 6, 8, 10, 12, 14, 16, 18 – Women

Women's 14w – 26w and 1X, 2X, 3X – Larger-sized women

Dresses and Suits

	Size										
USA	4	6	8	10	12	14	16	18	20	22	24	26
UK	6	8	10	12	14	16	18	20	22	24	26	28
European	34	36	38	40	42	44	46	48	50	52	54	56

Clothing Size Chart

Shoes

	Size						
USA	6	6 ½	7	7 ½	8	8 ½	
UK	4 ½	5	5 ½	6	6 ½	7	
European	38	38	39	39	40	41	

Men's Clothing

Suits and Coats

	Size						
USA	36	38	40	42	44	46	48
UK	36	38	40	42	44	46	48
European	46	48	50	52	54	56	58

Shirts

	Size						
USA	14	14 ½	15	15 ½	16	16 ½	17
UK	14	14 ½	15	15 ½	16	16 ½	17
European	36	37	38	39	41	42	43

Shoes

	Size								
USA	8	8 ½	9	9 ½	10	10 ½	11	11 ½	12
UK	7	7 ½	8	8 ½	9	9 ½	10	10 ½	11
European	41	42		43		44		45	46

Children's Clothing

Infants – newborn to 24 months

Toddlers – 1T - 4T

Children – 5 - 12

USA	4	6	8	10	12
UK	43	48	55	58	60
European	125	135	150	155	160

Summary

There are many places to shop in America. The choices can make it confusing. Take the time to learn your shopping area and choose the types of stores you are most comfortable with. Managing your money, comparing prices, understanding the sales tax and knowing the value of different quality is very important.

Once you understand the basic guidelines, shopping in America can be a fun experience. Many people in America shop for goods just for fun! If you understand the value of your money, you can become an informed consumer.

Glossary

Bar code: a marking printed on the label of a product to identify it and allow faster calculation of prices by the store register. Also known as a Universal Product Code (UPC).

Catalog: a magazine or book containing pictures of, and information on, items being sold by a merchant along with directions on how to place an order with the merchant.

Consumers: the people who buy goods and services.

Convenience store: a small store, often attached to a gas station, that concentrates on selling a selection of essential items for the convenience of their customers.

Coupon: a small certificate, issued by a store or manufacturer, offering a product at a reduced price as an incentive to buy that product or shop in that store.

Department store: a store that sells a wide variety of non-food items.

Discount store: a store that concentrates on selling a selection of products at a lower price.

Drugstore/Pharmacy: a smaller store featuring a pharmacy for buying prescription drugs.

Exchange rate: the cost or benefit of exchanging the currency of your country for American money.

Farmer's Market: a small group of farmers who sell fresh produce at a shared location.

Flea Market: a big yard sale in a specific location, where individual people set up an area and sell their items.

Garage Sale/Yard Sale: a sale held by individuals or neighborhoods in their garages or yards.

National brands: products sold throughout America under a single company's name.

Outlet Mall/Factory Outlet: a large outdoor shopping mall selling merchandise at a discounted price.

Shopping Mall: a large group of specialty stores and department stores together in one location.

Specialty store: a store that specializes in a particular product.

Store brands/Generic brands: products that are similar to national brand products, but are sold by each store under its own name (store brands) or no name at all (generic brands).

Strip Mall: a small group of specialty stores in a row.

Supermarket/Grocery Store: a store that sells food and household products.

Superstore: a combination of a grocery store and department store.

Tipping: giving someone an additional amount of money, called a "tip" or "gratuity," for service they have provided or for doing an exceptional job.

Unit price: the price of a product based on the weight or quantity purchased.

Warranty: a guarantee by the company to repair or replace defective items for a certain period of time after purchase.

Wholesale club: a members-only club located in a large warehouse featuring bulk (large-sized) quantities of products at a discounted price.

Exercises

1. Internet Exercise (see Pages 211-212 for more information on the Internet): Log on to any search engine (www.google.com, www.dogpile.com, www.yahoo.com) and search by the following terms to learn more about shopping and the value of money. For many of these, you may choose to put the name of the city or state you live in before the word or phrase. Doing this will bring up local information as well as national information.

   - Better Business Bureau
   - Supermarkets
   - Superstores
   - Pharmacies
   - Malls
   - Factory outlets
   - The value of money
   - International exchange rate
   - Sales tax
   - Bartering
   - National brands
   - Sales
   - Clothing
   - Clothing sizes
   - Catalogs
   - Online stores

2. Buy your local Sunday paper. In it, you will find several ads and coupons for different food items. Plan a meal with a few friends and see who can buy all the ingredients for the least amount of money (who can save the most). This exercise can be fun and feed you as well!

Chapter 9

Dining In, Dining Out

Nowhere is the presence of different cultures in the United States as obvious as in the foods we eat. It is true that America is known for its fast-food – McDonald's and Coca-Cola. With the busy lives and fast pace of the American lifestyle, convenience foods are popular for many people, and many Americans go to restaurants to eat as often as two to three times a week.

Grocery Shopping

You can buy food, along with household supplies, in many locations. You can choose to shop at a big supermarket, a large warehouse, or at a local grocery or convenience store down the street. As you become familiar with the area you live in, you will become familiar with the stores that have what you need.

Ask co-workers, friends, and neighbors for places to shop. Someone who has lived in the area for a long time will often know the best places to find the foods you want at the cheapest prices. Remember, larger stores may have more selection at a lower cost than smaller stores, but the smaller stores may have better service and more specialty items.

Ethnic Groceries

In many larger cities and towns, you will be able to find small ethnic grocery stores specializing in the food and supplies of a specific country or region of the world. Look in the phone book or ask your friends and neighbors if they can recommend any specialty groceries.

> **In This Chapter**
> - Food shopping
> - Eating out is a type of American entertainment
> - Dining in American restaurants
> - Tipping is expected
> - American manners and etiquette

Health Food Stores

A **health food store** is a specialty shop that focuses on natural healing and health. Health food stores sell vitamins, herbs, mineral supplements, and wholesome foods. Many Americans are concerned about the chemicals and preservatives often used to grow and preserve the foods we eat. Health food stores often feature organic foods. Organic foods are foods grown without the use of chemicals, pesticides, and other potentially harmful substances. Health food stores may also have more ethnic foods and more locally raised fruits and vegetables.

Meat, Poultry, and Fish

Fresh meat, poultry, and fish are widely available throughout the United States. Many of the animals are raised in the United States. The government strictly regulates quality control. The major sources of meat in the United States include:

- Beef (from cattle)
- Chicken
- Pork (from hogs and pigs)
- Fish
- Lamb (sheep).

Most supermarkets and grocery stores have meat departments where you can purchase prepackaged meats. Some stores have a butcher who can cut the meat to your liking.

Meats can be purchased prepackaged or freshly cut.

The United States has high standards for preparing and storing meat products. There are many federal and state rules regarding its preparation. Most meat products have storage and handling information printed on the label. All meat, poultry, and fish have storage expiration dates. For the freshest foods, don't use them past the expiration date listed on the product.

Fruits and Vegetables

One of the things many immigrants like about American grocery stores is the wide variety of fresh fruits and vegetables available. California, Texas, and Florida are the three states that provide much of our fresh produce year-round. The United States also imports many fruit and vegetable products from around the world.

Like our meats, fresh fruits and vegetables must also pass strict government guidelines before they can be sold in stores. It is a good idea to wash all fruits and vegetables before eating them. Washing them with water will remove dirt, chemicals, and preservatives.

Farmer's markets and produce stands are often found in the summer months, and year-round in warmer climates. These outdoor markets feature locally grown fresh produce.

Prepackaged Foods

Some Americans don't have the time or desire to cook meals. Some people may not even know how to cook meals. Americans are often looking for ways to make things faster and more convenient. This includes the food they eat. Many of the foods we eat are pre-prepared by food companies. They often freeze or can entire meals that can be heated and eaten at a later time. Most meals can be heated in an oven, on the stove or range, or in the microwave.

A microwave is a common appliance found in most homes. It is used to thaw and cook food rapidly. A meal that might take an hour to prepare may take only 8 to 10 minutes in a microwave. Read the preparation instructions on the package of the food to see if it can be heated in the microwave.

While prepackaged foods are convenient, they are usually full of fat, salt, and ingredients to preserve the food. The quality and taste of pre-prepared foods may not be as good as a fully prepared meal using fresh ingredients, but the time savings in cooking and serving the meal is valued.

Microwaves are a fast way to heat and reheat foods.

Dining Out—Eating Out

Every immigrant in the history of the United States has brought his or her own traditions and tastes to America. America offers a wide variety of restaurants and foods from all over the world. In fact, many immigrants work by opening restaurants specializing in the food of their native countries. In any city you will find ethnic restaurants. Depending on the cultures in the region, you will find different foods. For example, if large populations of Hispanic workers come to a city for jobs, you will see restaurants that feature the food of that culture.

Today, ethnic restaurants are more common than in the past. Twenty years ago, while it wasn't unusual to find authentic Mexican cuisine in the Southwest or in large cities, Mexican style food was hard to find elsewhere in the country. The same was true of other ethnic foods. Today, Americans are enjoying foods from around the world. Even in the Midwest, often the last part of the country to feel new influences, you can find Italian, Mexican, American, Greek, Indian, Thai, Japanese, Korean, Mandarin, Mongolian, and Middle Eastern styles of food, to name a few.

Ethnic restaurants are popular in America.

Types of Restaurants

Different restaurants offer various styles, or ways, of eating. Some of the most popular styles include:

Fast-food – Quick service, limited selection, low cost – you can go in and eat, go through a drive-through in your car and pick it up, or carry it out.

Delivery – You place an order by phone and your food is delivered to your home.

Sit-down dining – Your food is served to you by a wait person at a restaurant.

Buffet – You pay a set price for as much food as you want to eat. You usually serve yourself.

Cafeteria – Each item is individually plated and priced. You select the items you want.

A basic place setting

The American Restaurant Experience

Here is a look at what to expect in an average American sit-down restaurant:

Drinks First

Depending on the restaurant, your server may bring ice water.

Most restaurants offer free refills on iced tea, soft drinks, and coffee.

Alcoholic Beverages – You must be at least 21 years old to drink liquor. You may be asked for identification to prove your age.

Your server will wait on you during the meal.

Appetizers

Usually small portions ordered before the meal. These items are optional and may be shared. Many appetizers are eaten with your fingers.

Nachos are a common appetizer.

Soup/Salad

A choice of soup or salad is often included with many dinners.

The salad is made of lettuce with some vegetable toppings and served with salad dressing (oil or mayonnaise based).

Entree

Main meal – usually contains meat, poultry, or fish; potatoes, pasta, or rice, and a vegetable.

Dessert

Usually sweet – ice cream, fruit, cake, or pie.

Cheeseburger, French fries and coleslaw with a pickle

Tipping

If you have had a sit-down meal where a waiter or waitress has served you, it is customary to give your server a tip. A tip of 15% to 20% of the total cost of the meal should be given to the server. **A tip is expected, it is not charity to the waiter, or begging, it is payment for their service.** Servers generally have lower wages and depend on tips to make their money. The better the service, the better the tip should be.

Some restaurants will automatically include a tip in the bill if there are more than seven or eight people at the table. If this is the case, you do not have to leave an additional tip. If you have trouble figuring out how much to tip, you can buy a tip table card to carry with you. A tip table shows meal ranges and the amount the tip should be at 15% or 20%.

If you are eating with several friends and you each want to pay for your own meals, you can tell your server you want separate bills (often called separate checks). Tell your server you want separate checks at the beginning of the meal.

If you have food delivered to your home or office, you should tip the driver. This is generally $1 to $2.

A tip table can help you figure how much tip to leave for your server.

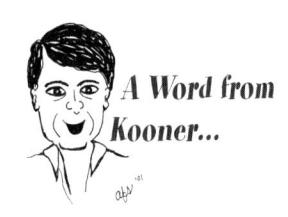

A Word from Kooner...

One thing about Americans is they often use the same word to describe different things. When I first came to America I was in a cafeteria and was commenting to an American friend about the "nice buns," or rolls, they were serving. He gave me a very strange look. When I told my brother about it later, he asked me where I was when I said that. He laughed and told me "buns" is a slang word for someone's rear end. Saying "nice buns..." was complimenting someone on the shape of their bottom!

Eating with Other People

Americans are often very casual about inviting people over for dinner and meals. It is not unusual for a friend to invite you over for dinner. Some may ask if you want to share a favorite food and help to make a meal. If you receive an invitation to dinner, it is always polite to bring a small gift to the host or hostess. The gift can be a bottle of wine, flowers, or a small gift that would please your friend. If you are not sure about what to do or wear, just ask. Most people want you to feel comfortable. You should plan to arrive on time. Do not be late!

Good Manners Are Important

When you are eating out or with friends it is important to behave properly. Here are some general rules for dining:

- ✦ Wait until everyone is served before beginning to eat.

Eating with Other People 117

- Eat quietly and keep your mouth closed when eating.
- Do not talk with your mouth full.
- Burping in the United States is not polite and is considered very rude. If you need to burp, cover your mouth and do it as quietly as possible. If you do burp, say, "Excuse me."
- Do not smoke at the table unless you are in a smoking section and everyone else has finished.
- Your napkin goes in your lap.
- Sit up straight, hands in your lap when you are not eating.

Use proper manners when dining.

- In a restaurant, it is appropriate to sit quietly, speak in a normal voice, not too loud (unless the music is loud!).
- You will use the silverware on the outside of the place setting first.
- Do not be afraid to try new things. Eat with the fork, cut with the knife or side of the fork, and use the spoon to eat anything served in a bowl.
- Do not use your napkin to blow your nose. Use it to wipe your mouth or hands and keep your hands clean.
- If there is something in the food you are allergic to or do not like, do not spit it out. Set the remaining food aside on your plate.

Eating Family Style

When you eat in someone's home or in some restaurants and the food is passed around the table, it is called eating **family style**. Some general guidelines include:

- Food is passed around the table following the guidelines of the host. If he or she passes dishes to the left, you do the same.
- Take a small helping of food and pass the dish on to the next person. Make sure there is enough for everyone to have some of each dish.

Family style meal

- It is not polite to ask for second helpings. If there is enough food for seconds, the host will offer it.
- If you did not get a certain dish, ask for it: "Please pass the rolls."
- It is impolite to reach across the table for anything. Ask someone to pass the dish.
- Some foods are eaten with your hands; others are not. Watch your host or hostess to see what they do.

Summary

There is a lot of variety in American food. You can enjoy fast-food, sit-down dining, and ethnic restaurants from all over the world. You can also stay home and make your own meals. Eating with friends, families and new acquaintances is a great way to relax and get to know other people. Americans see eating as a social, relaxing experience. Enjoy!

Glossary

Buffet: a restaurant where, for a set price, you may take as much food as you want to eat. In general, you may take food only for yourself and unfinished food may not be taken home.

Cafeteria: a restaurant where each item is individually plated and priced. You select the items you want.

Delivery: you place an order by phone and your food is delivered to your home.

Family style eating: where food is passed around the table.

Fast-food: a restaurant specializing in quick service of a limited selection of items at a low cost. Food may be eaten in the restaurant, carried out or you may go through a drive-through lane in your car.

Health food store: a specialty shop that focuses on natural healing and health, selling vitamins, herbs, mineral supplements, and wholesome foods.

Sit-down dining: a restaurant where you tell a server what items you want and he or she brings your meal from the kitchen to your table when it is ready. In general, unfinished food may be boxed up for you to take home.

Tipping: giving someone an additional amount of money, called a "tip" or "gratuity," for service they have provided or for doing an exceptional job.

Exercise

1. Internet Exercise (see Pages 211-212 for more information on the Internet): Log on to any search engine (www.google.com, www.dogpile.com, www.yahoo.com) and search by the following terms to learn more about restaurants and manners. For many of these, you may choose to put the name of the city or state you live in before the word or phrase. Doing this will bring up local information as well as national information.

- Supermarkets
- Picking good produce
- How to get a deal
- Ethnic food stores
- Health food stores
- Picking good meats and poultry
- Restaurants
- National Restaurant Association
- Types of dining
- Eating out in America
- How to tip in America
- Tip chart
- Proper manners
- Proper etiquette
- Family style eating.

2. In Chapter 9 you planned a meal with your friends. Now prepare the meal together and have a sit-down dinner. This dinner will have a twist though. Correct each other on any bad manners you see. Include things such as elbows on the table, posture, and courtesy.

Chapter 10

Out on Your Own

Becoming successful and having the ability to be independent are two goals most Americans strive for. America allows you to choose how you wish to pursue success and independence. It is much easier to learn new things when you have a person to help you.

Agreements with Your Mentor

Many people seek out a mentor when coming to the United States. A **mentor** is someone you trust who can give you advice on your new experiences. You will want to find a mentor who can help you quickly adjust to American ways.

Many people use a friend or relative as a mentor. Other people who come to the United States and do not know anyone may try to connect with a religious or social group to find a mentor. You may have several mentors during your first year. The feedback and guidance you will get from your mentor may save you time, money, and hardship.

Am I a Guest or Family?

Many new immigrants live with their mentors for a period of time. The biggest question most need to address with their mentors is, "Am I a guest?" It is important to have an agreement for your mentor's help. We often treat guests more formally than we would a member of the family. We may also expect different things from family members and friends. Setting up guidelines before you arrive can help make things go better.

> **In This Chapter**
> - Living with your mentor
> - Getting to know people
> - Setting and achieving personal goals
> - Living on your own

How Long to Stay?

If you are staying with your mentor, it is important the length of your stay be very clearly stated. Discuss in advance how long you will live with the mentor or a family. A reasonable amount of time for you to arrange for your own living space is within the first year. This may be influenced by the amount of money being saved or the amount of time on the job. Whatever your choice, be sure everything is agreeable to everyone involved.

You may choose to make a list of goals you want to reach before you move out on your own. Set timelines for achieving your goals. Some of your goals may be:

✦ The amount of money you want to earn

✦ The length of time you want to work at a job

✦ A specific calendar date

✦ Being able to speak English

✦ Learning the transportation system

✦ Making new friends.

	1st Month	2nd Month	3rd Month	4th Month	5th Month	6th Month
Get social security card	X					
Open bank account	X					
Shop for groceries	X					
Read newspaper in English		X				
Get a job			X			
Look for housing				X	X	
Drive a car						X

Create a plan of when you want to achieve certain goals.

Paying Your Way

Some people come to this country with few belongings and very little money. Other people come to the United States with a lot of belongings and plenty of money. When you are making agreements with your mentor, you should include a list of expenses you will help to pay, such as food, clothing, utilities, phone calls, etc. The more specific you are about expenses and responsibilities you will take on, the more successful your partnership with your mentor will be.

List of Expenses to Discuss

- Food and supplies
- Hygiene and grooming
- Transportation, like a car or bus
- Telephone use
- Dining out
- Clothing
- Insurance
- Travel.

Decide ahead of time what expenses you will pay.

A Word from Kooner...

When my nephew came to live with me, we agreed he would stay with me for a one-year time period. I did not charge him for rent or utilities. As soon as he got a job, he bought his own stuff like food and clothing. I think it is OK to talk about bills and expenses. It is good to discuss how much they are and how often you pay them. I did not make my nephew pay half of the bills, but as he got on his feet he did pay a part of them we had agreed upon. Some of the bills he was completely responsible for. The long-distance telephone bill stands out as the one bill the person needs to pay in total.

Mixing and Mingling

One of the best ways to transition into the American way of life is to meet people. Often men, women, and families with the same religious beliefs or social practices are the easiest to get to know. Places of worship, such as churches, synagogues, temples, and mosques are good places to start. You could meet a mentor there who will help show you around the area or find a job or housing.

Finding other groups can help you get to know America as well. It is good to have something to do and people to talk to. These groups can be involved in sports or other hobbies. This is one way you can network to make new friends and to build new relationships. Another word for social groups may be "clubs" or "associations."
Ask around or check out the Internet for your local listings.

Get to know people by joining groups.

Making Your Own Decisions

There are many choices you will need to make now that you have come to a new country. The next few pages will discuss some ways to make decisions and how to set and achieve goals.

Setting Goals—Making It Happen

The first part of good decision-making is to know what you want. When starting out, it is always important to have a **goal**. A goal is the skill, event, or object you want to achieve. Basically, a goal is something you want.

A couple of examples could be ... Take classes to learn English ... or Own my own restaurant.

Organize your goals into short-term and long-term goals. Short-term goals are goals you may need to achieve quickly. Long-term goals could take several years to accomplish.

For example, a short-term goal may be to find a way to get to work. Long-term goals could include owning your own business or getting a degree or certification.

Place your long-term goals to be achieved in one-year, two-years, or five-year lists. It is helpful to try to decide how you want your life to be in one year, two years, five years, etc. You may find it helpful to write out your goals for reference.

For example, within the first year of living in the United States, you may want to take English as a second language class (ESL), buy a car, etc. Your two- to five-year goals, or long-term goal, may include wanting to save enough money for a down payment on a house; or to start your own business.

Setting Career Goals—Try to decide what goals you want to achieve in your career.

For example, a career goal could be to become a manager within three years of working for a company.

Getting a Plan—How You Will Achieve Your Goals

Identify the steps you will need to complete in order to achieve your goal. Setting steps for reaching your goal will make it easier to achieve.

For example, what will it take to be able to study English in a class?

- Locate classes, including the cost and schedule of classes
- Coordinate the classes with your work schedule; the times and dates
- Identify how to sign up and pay for classes
- Secure transportation to classes
- Examine each step toward your goal. Are there smaller parts of each step?

For example, if you want to be a department leader at work, you may need more education, to gain experience in all the parts of the department, to gain management experience, and decide when would be best to apply for the position.

Write down the steps of the process. Decide on a timeline for each of the steps to be achieved. Organize your plan by daily and weekly goals. It is often very helpful to write about these activities.

Ask for suggestions on your plan. You may find it helpful to ask your mentor for ideas about your goals.

Getting What You Need

Now that you have a plan to achieve your goal, you will need to get the materials and resources necessary to achieve the goal.

Make a list of any items or resources you may need and the cost of each. These items or resources can be:

- Time
- Money
- Goods and services.

When you make a list of resources it is important to decide on the cost of each item. Even if the item is your time, it is still important to plan for that time. The time you may need to accomplish your goal may impact what type of job you can have. Whatever the expense, you will need to estimate the cost of getting what you need and then obtain it.

Moving Out on Your Own

Now that you have spent time with your mentor and have begun to adjust to your new way of life in America, you will need to prepare to live in your own home or apartment.

Affording It All

How do you know how much you can afford to spend on rent or a house payment? Start by making a complete list of your expenses. Plan on the following expenses:

- Rent or mortgage payment
- Utilities (electricity, gas, water, sewage, etc.)
- Local telephone service
- Long-distance telephone service
- Transportation expenses
- Food
- Dining out
- Insurance
- Clothing
- Entertainment
- Loan payment
- Credit card payments.

Make a budget to manage your money.

Next, you need to create a budget. A **budget** is a monthly spending plan based on your income and expenses. Determine how much money you make in a month. This is your income. List how much you will pay in expenses. Refer to the list above to help you list your expenses. If you are not sure how much you will pay for an expense, try to estimate an amount. Subtract your expenses from income. The remaining amount is the money you have left to spend or save. This is your budget! Be sure to spend your money the way you have planned.

It is very important to discuss finances, even when going out to dinner. Have fun with it! Who is buying the meal? Will someone pay for the entire check? It may be hard the first time you try it, but it is important to understand. Take the pleasant approach. The mentor may treat you to dinner at a sit-down restaurant and then you treat your mentor to dinner at the fast-food places.

Summary

You are ready to start the process to becoming independent. You may choose to live with someone when you first move to America, however, you will eventually want to move out on your own. You need to take the time to learn how to budget your money so you may become independent. Use your budget to help set realistic goals and timelines for achieving your independence.

Use the chapters of this book to get you started. Remember there are also hundreds of resources you can rely on for help. The local library and the Internet have places to help you!

Glossary

Budget: a monthly spending plan based on your income and expenses.

Goal: a skill, event, or object that you want to achieve.

Mentor: someone you trust who can give you advice on your new experiences.

Exercises

1. Internet Exercise (see Pages 211-212 for more information on the Internet): Log on to any search engine (www.google.com, www.dogpile.com, www.yahoo.com) and search by the following terms to learn more about getting out on your own. For many of these, you may choose to put the name of the city or state you live in before the word or phrase. Doing this will bring up local information as well as national information.

   - Welcome Wagon
   - Newcomers
   - Social organizations
   - Goal setting and planning
   - Moving.

2. Set yourself a goal you would like to achieve within the next year. Develop a plan for how you are going to achieve your goal. For example, if you want to own a car, what type of things do you have to do to be able to get that car . . . save enough money, get a license, learn to drive, or whatever you may need to do to achieve your goal. The goal can be simple or complex; it just has to be something you want to do!

Chapter 11

Balancing Home and Work

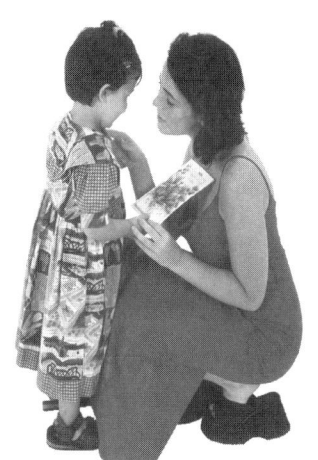

Many Americans choose to work at more than one job in order to live the way they want. In many families, both spouses are working full time. It can be a challenge to make money and be successful while trying to take care of a home and a family. Being successful personally will help you be more confident on the job. This chapter will discuss these types of issues for families in America.

Taking Care of Your Family

In many countries, children are raised by their parents and by extended families. An **extended family** is a family that has parents, grandparents, aunts, uncles, brothers, sisters, and children all living in the same, or in nearby, homes. Very few American families are extended families.

Americans are a very mobile society. Many people choose to move to different towns, cities, or regions many times during their lives. Members of American families may move to areas of the country far from other family members. In the United States many families use close friends as their extended family.

Whether you are married and have children, are a single parent, or are planning to start a family, it is important your children be taken care of while you are at work. There are many choices for working parents including:

- ✦ Childcare
- ✦ Day care
- ✦ Preschool
- ✦ After school programs.

> **IN THIS CHAPTER**
> - Caring for your family
> - Medical care options
> - Safety and security
> - Understanding time
> - Holidays and traditions of America
> - Vacationing in the United States

Childcare

Parents, grandparents, other family members, or friends can play a role in childcare. Some people choose to have child-care professionals come to their home. A child-care professional who comes to your home is called a "nanny" or "baby sitter." It is important you know and trust the person you choose as a nanny or baby sitter.

Day Care

A **day care** is a company licensed to watch children. Typically, you would leave your children at a day-care center while you are at work. The children are supervised by trained adults and are with other children of varying ages.

Finding a good day care center can be challenging. Things to consider when looking for a day-care center include:

- Quality of reputation
- Cleanliness
- Number of children each teacher has to care for
- Ages of the other children attending the day care center
- Number of certified teachers at the day care
- Location of the day-care center
- Record of safety for the day-care center.

If your child is sick—In most day-care centers, if your child is ill, has a high body temperature, or diarrhea (loose bowel movements), the day-care center may send your child home. Depending on their regulations, you may not be able to take your child back to school for 48 hours to help prevent infecting other children with bacteria and germs.

Children at play

Preschool

Preschool is a school-style day care for children between the ages of 3 and 6. The teachers work with children in classrooms. The class activities are designed to prepare children for school.

After School Programs

Working parents of school-age children may find school is over before the end of their workday. Finding care for your children between the hours school ends and the time you come home can be a challenge. To help with this, many schools and community centers offer "after school programs."

Children who are in an "after school program" are supervised by a teacher after the end of the regular school day. Children can work on homework assignments or play with other children. You may have to pay for using this program.

Care of the Elderly

Caring for elderly or disabled parents can be very similar to caring for children. This is difficult for many working families. There are many care options available for the elderly. Some elderly care options include:

- Senior day-care centers
- Nursing homes
- Retirement homes or communities
- Assisted living facilities.

A **senior day-care center** is a facility with trained staff that assists the participant in daily activities outside their home. **Nursing homes** provide living arrangements and care for the elderly or chronically ill and individuals recovering from surgery or injuries. **Retirement homes or communities** are housing complexes where an elderly person who has retired from their life's work may choose to live. Some retirement homes offer on-site nursing as well.

In an **assisted living facility**, the elderly person lives in a hotel-type setting that is attached to, or near a care facility. They can live independently with some daily or weekly assistance as needed.

Some families choose to use private nurse services. A nurse may come into your home every day or live in your home to care for the elderly person. Private nurse care can be very expensive.

When Someone Is Sick

What should you do when your child or someone else in your family is sick? If the child or family member needs immediate medical attention, you should be sure they receive appropriate medical attention by taking them to the nearest emergency room. If the situation is not dangerous, you should call your family doctor and set up an appointment for them.

You may need to stay home to care for the sick person. If this is the case, you will need to communicate with your boss. Explain the situation to your supervisor. Most employers are willing to adjust your schedule so you can care for a sick family member. Check your company benefits. Your organization may provide sick days, health days, or personal days you can use when you or your family member is sick.

Medical Care In America

It is important to remember the government does not pay for your medical expenses. You are responsible for paying for yourself and your family's medical expenses. Having medical insurance is a way many people manage their medical expenses. Like automobile or home insurance, you must pay a premium for medical insurance. Many employers offer health care as a benefit.

There are several different choices you have when you or your family gets sick. Your choices can include:

+ Doctor's office
+ "Immediate care" or "prompt care" medical centers
+ Clinics
+ Hospital emergency rooms.

Having health insurance can save you money on medical bills.

The Doctor's Office

You should choose a family doctor whenever you move to a new area. If you have health insurance, your health insurance company may specify which doctors you can visit. Follow their guidelines in order to avoid additional charges from your insurance company. Once you have a list of doctors your insurance company will allow you to use, you will want to choose a family physician, or **general practitioner** (GP). A GP is a doctor who has general knowledge of medicine and can give care for the most common illnesses. Ask your friends or co-workers for advice on the doctors in the area to help you make your decision.

When you or a family member gets sick, you should visit your family doctor first. Your family doctor may choose to send you to a specialist. A **specialist** is a doctor who has had additional training in a particular area of medicine. Some examples of specialists in particular areas include:

- Pediatrician: children's health
- ENT: ear, nose, and throat
- Podiatrist: feet
- **Internist**: internal organs
- **Gerontologist**: the health of the elderly.

You should visit your doctor for routine checkups. Many doctors have very busy schedules. You may need to make an appointment a few weeks in advance of the time you want to go for your checkup.

Schedule regular medical checkups.

For emergency situations, you can try to get an appointment immediately. Most doctor offices set aside a certain amount of time each day for emergency appointments. If your doctor does not have any available appointments, and your health concern is serious, your doctor may direct you to go to the emergency room of a hospital, or to an urgent care facility.

Clinics and Walk-in Medical Center

A **clinic** is a medical office with a group of doctors. When you visit a clinic, you will not have an assigned doctor. The first available doctor will treat you.

A Walk-in medical center is a medical office you can visit without an appointment. You wait your turn to see a doctor. Most walk-in offices are open in the evenings.

The Hospital/Emergency Room

If you have an emergency situation and you need to see a doctor immediately, you can go to the emergency room at a local hospital. Some examples of emergency situations can include:

- You think you have a broken bone
- You have serious injuries

You do not need an appointment at an immediate care office.

- You have been poisoned
- You are critically ill
- You have been in an accident.

In these situations, and any time you feel as though your situation cannot wait, you need to get help as soon as possible. A hospital **emergency room** is equipped to care for people with serious health needs.

Emergency room treatment can be very expensive, and only some treatments may be covered by insurance. An emergency room should only be used for extremely serious injuries or illnesses. An emergency room will treat anyone, regardless of his or her ability to pay. However, if you visit an emergency room and do not have insurance, you will be responsible for the bill.

Surgery and Outpatient Surgery

Surgery is a medical procedure done by a doctor to treat an injury or disease. A surgery, after which you go home, rather than remaining in the hospital, is known as **outpatient surgery**. You go to the hospital in the morning as an outpatient. You have your surgery or procedure done and return home that evening.

Many medical procedures have become more advanced. Procedures that used to require a long hospital stay for recovery are now done as outpatient surgery.

Pre-Approval

Many insurance companies require non-emergency surgeries and hospital stays be **pre-approved or pre-admitted**. You or your doctor would need to contact the insurance company for approval of the procedure or stay. If this is not done, the insurance company may not pay the hospital bill.

Co-pay

In many cases, the insurance company will pay for most of the cost of the visit or medication, and you will be asked to pay for a small portion of it. A **co-pay** is a portion of the bill you need to pay when visiting the doctor or buying medicine.

Prescription Drugs

Prescription drugs are medicines your doctor will tell you to take for specific medical conditions. These drugs can only be purchased with a doctor's authorization. Your doctor will give you a note called a prescription. You can take the prescription to any pharmacy. The pharmacist will fill, or process the prescription, and package it for you. The pharmacist will give you instructions on how to use the medicine. It is important you do not share prescription medicines with others. Remember to take all of the prescribed medicine.

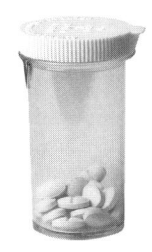

Prescription medication is purchased at a pharmacy.

Dentist and Dental Care

Dentists and dental clinics take care of your teeth. Most dental insurance plans pay for the majority of the cost of routine cleaning and X-rays. Routine cleaning should be done every six months. Some other dental procedures can include:

- Filling cavities
- Pulling teeth
- Crowns
- Bridges
- Root canals.

If surgery is required, your dentist may need to send you to an oral surgeon. **Oral surgeons** usually have special equipment and facilities for surgical procedures. Oral surgeons have more training than dentists. Oral surgery is usually performed on an outpatient basis.

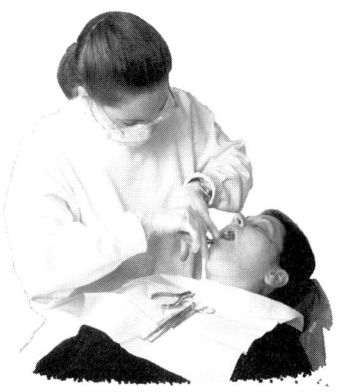

Many companies offer dental care insurance.

Eye Care

You will need to visit an eye doctor's office if you are having problems with your eyes. An eye doctor's office is a place where you can go to get glasses or have your eyes examined for health. There are two types of eye doctors:

- **Optometrists** are licensed to do eye exams and prescribe eyeglasses and contact lenses
- **Ophthalmologists** do eye surgery in addition to standard eye exams and care.

Vision care insurance is usually separate from medical insurance. You may choose not to carry vision insurance if you have never experienced eye problems.

Many companies offer vision insurance.

Immunizations and Preventative Drugs

Most Americans have their children immunized against disease. Day cares and schools require them before your child can be enrolled. An **immunization** is an injection of medication that helps the body protect itself from diseases. Immunizations are made to combat specific diseases. Some common immunizations are:

- Tetanus
- Measles
- Mumps
- Rubella
- Polio.

Minimum Immunization Requirements

- Three doses of tetanus and diphtheria, usually received as DPT, DT, OR Td vaccine
- Three doses of polio vaccine

It has also become popular for Americans to get annual influenza and pneumonia immunizations. These can help prevent the flu and cold-like symptoms.

To maintain U.S. health standards, children are required to receive certain immunizations to attend school. The following chart shows some of the immunizations required.

It is important to have a record of your child's immunizations. All states now require proof of immunization before they will allow children to attend school. You can get specific information on immunization requirements from your doctor or school.

Every doctor's office offers immunization shots. State laws vary regarding what immunizations are needed. The majority of states require proof your child has received the minimum requirements. If you do not have a doctor or cannot afford a doctor, contact your state Board of Health office. Most states offer immunizations free of charge.

If you plan on traveling to certain countries, you are required to receive a series of immunization shots before leaving the United States. This is to protect you and others when you return.

Over-the-Counter Drugs

Another term you will encounter in America is over-the-counter drugs. These are medicines you can purchase without a doctor's prescription. Examples of a few of these might be:

- Aspirin
- Tylenol/ibuprofen
- Laxatives
- Cough medicines
- Cold tablets
- Sinus medication.

Natural Remedies

Some people use natural, or homeopathic, remedies. Natural remedies and supplements to help prevent illness are becoming more popular in America. Health food stores that specialize in natural supplements and vitamins are available in most cities. Many of these natural remedies have not been approved by the FDA (the Federal Food and Drug Administration) or not regulated by the government. This means the quality and effectiveness of the ingredients in these medicines cannot be guaranteed.

Safety and Security

Safety and security is important to people in the United States. Several choices go into being safe and keeping your family secure.

Keeping Yourself and Your Family Safe

Using common sense helps to keep you safe.

To keep your home safe:

- Lock the windows and doors of your home at night and when you leave
- Stop your mail and newspapers when on vacation
- Rotate the lights you leave on at night with timers when you are not at home.

To keep safe on the streets and in your car:

- Lock your car when you get out
- Do not leave children or pets in your car
- Avoid high crime areas
- Pay attention to your surroundings and avoid situations that are risky
- Do not walk alone after dark or in poorly lit areas.

Defending Yourself

There are times in spite of your best efforts crime finds you. You have the right to protect yourself, but there are laws which govern how.

Firearms—If you decide to buy a gun, a firearm permit is required. There are additional laws about ammunition and the waiting periods on buying a gun. In the United States, there are also laws about carrying your weapon on your body where it cannot be seen. Check your local laws when applying for a firearm permit.

Gangs—Some communities have trouble with gang violence. **Gangs** are groups of people (usually youths) who stake out territory and rights in an area. The local, state, and federal laws are in place to handle gangs. Many communities have programs to give children a chance for alternate activities.

Violent Crimes—Can still happen to you. Having good street smarts (judgment about safety and security on the streets) is how you avoid becoming a victim of crime. It is important to learn when to call for help and how to protect yourself. The best way to stay safe is to avoid those areas that have high crime. Should you become a victim of crime, you need to cooperate fully with the police, fire and emergency staff when the reports are being taken. If court action is taken, police and hospital records are important evidence.

When You Have an Emergency

Dialing 911—In the United States, there is a nearly universal system for calling for help: dial 9-1-1. This works on regular telephones and cell phones. Always give your name, location, and what the emergency is you are calling to report. You will speak to an operator who will dispatch the police, fire, and/or ambulance to your location.

Police—The **police department**, also known as law enforcement officers, are responsible for maintaining order, enforcing laws, and preventing and detecting crime. In the United States, these are trusted men and women who serve either at a community, state, or federal level.

Fire Department—The **fire department** is the local government department responsible for preventing and putting out fires. Often they also deal with chemical hazards and rescues requiring extension

Police officers protect citizens and enforce laws.

ladders. The fire department works the police department and the emergency agencies.

Emergency Medical Team—The **emergency medical team**, also known as EMTs, staff an ambulance that answers calls for health emergencies. The ambulance will take the victim to the nearest hospital emergency room (ER).

All three departments, police, fire, and emergency, cooperate and are coordinated through the 911-phone system. Calling 911 rather than the direct line to the police, fire, and emergency departments can save critical time in an emergency.

Understanding Time in America

Americans are very time conscious. Most Americans work the same schedule every day. Employers expect you to be on time when you are scheduled to work. It is important to be on time for social activities as well. Concerts and movies start at specific times, and it is impolite to arrive late.

Americans are time conscious.

A Word from Kooner...

For a while I was having a really hard time waking up on time in the morning. I had even been late for work a few times. My mother decided to help! The next time I was late, and hadn't gotten up, she dumped cold water on me in bed! After that, I suddenly had a reason to get up on time!

Holidays and Traditions

America is a nation of people from many different cultures. Our holidays reflect the varied traditions of our people. You may find it helpful to know about the holidays celebrated in the United States.

American Holidays

In America, we have 10 federal U.S. holidays, where all local, state, and federal government offices are closed. Many of these holidays are celebrated on a Monday or Friday, regardless of the actual holiday date, so people can enjoy a three-day weekend. Many businesses follow the same holiday schedule. These holidays include:

Holiday	Explanation
New Year's Day (January 1)	Celebrating the first day of the new calendar year.
Martin Luther King Jr. Day (Second week in January)	To commemorate and celebrate the life and birthday of Dr. Martin Luther King Jr., a civil rights leader.
President's Day (third week in February)	This day honors the Presidents of the United States.
Memorial Day (last Monday in May)	A patriotic day to honor American soldiers who have given their lives for the United States.
Independence Day (July 4)	Sometimes known as the Fourth of July, this holiday celebrates the signing of the Declaration of Independence and the founding of the United States.
Labor Day (First Monday in September)	This holiday is dedicated to the social and economic achievements of American workers. It is a yearly national tribute to the contributions workers have made to the prosperity and well-being of our country.
Columbus Day (Second week in October)	Columbus Day is now observed in all except nine states (and Washington, D.C.). In three states, it is known as Discovery Day, and in Michigan, it is known as Landing Day. It celebrates the day the explorer Christopher Columbus discovered America.
Veterans Day (Third week in November)	Formerly Armistice Day, Veterans Day is observed annually in the United States in honor of all those, living and dead, who served with the U.S. armed forces in wartime.

Holiday	Explanation
Thanksgiving Day (fourth Thursday in November)	A day of celebration and giving thanks. This day has its origin as a feast day during a celebration of harvest and friendship between the European settlers, or Pilgrims, and Native Americans.
Christmas (December 25)	Based on a celebration of the birth of Jesus in the Christian faith, it has come to be a time to give gifts and celebrate being with family and friends.

Other Holidays

In addition to our federal holidays, there are several other holidays Americans celebrate. Not everyone takes these days off from work, but they have become customs in our culture. Some of these days include:

Holiday	Explanation
Valentine's Day (February 14)	A day to send cards and flowers to someone you love.
St. Patrick's Day (March 17)	A holiday celebrating the Irish and their traditions.
Earth Day (April 22)	A day to remind us of the importance of taking care of the earth.
Secretaries' Day (April 24)	A day that recognizes secretaries and support staff who work at companies.
Mother's Day (Second Sunday in May)	A special day to celebrate mothers. Cards, flowers, etc., are often given.
Flag Day (June 14)	A day of respect and commemoration of the American flag.
Father's Day (Second Sunday in June)	A special day to celebrate fathers. Cards, gifts, etc., are often given.

Holiday	Explanation
Grandparents' Day (September 9)	A special day to celebrate grandparents. Cards, flowers, gifts, etc., are often exchanged.
National Children's Day (October 14)	A day to remind us how valuable children are.
National Boss Day (October 16)	A day dedicated to recognizing our bosses.
Sweetest Day (October 20)	Like Valentine's Day, a day to celebrate love and romance.
Halloween (October 31)	Halloween celebrations feature costumes and carved pumpkins. Costumed children go from house to house to receive candy.
Kwanzaa (Dec. 26-Jan. 1)	A holiday celebrating the African-American family and their traditions.

There may also be personal holidays or holidays specific to your country that you celebrate. Your boss may not be aware of your holidays. If you need the day off to celebrate your holiday, talk to your boss.

Religious Holidays

There are holidays also celebrated in America that are related to religions or religious practices. In this country, there are many different types of religions practiced. Some commonly observed religious holidays include: Ash Wednesday, Palm Sunday, Passover, Good Friday, Orthodox Holy Friday, Easter, Rosh Hashanah, Yom Kippur, Hanukkah, Ramadan, and Christmas. If you need time off for a religious holiday, talk with your boss.

Special Events

In addition to all the holidays mentioned, there are certain events in life that are celebrated in America. These include:

✦ Birthdays
✦ Graduation from high school and college
✦ Anniversaries, including wedding anniversaries, years worked, etc.

- ✦ Weddings
- ✦ Birth of a baby
- ✦ Funerals
- ✦ Religious events (examples include first Communion, Confirmation, Bar Mitzvah, Bat Mitzvah, etc.).

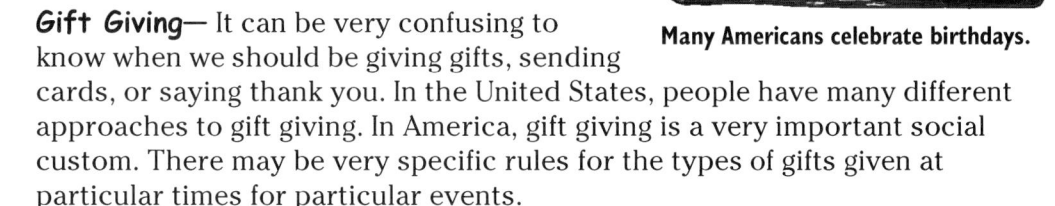

Many Americans celebrate birthdays.

Gift Giving— It can be very confusing to know when we should be giving gifts, sending cards, or saying thank you. In the United States, people have many different approaches to gift giving. In America, gift giving is a very important social custom. There may be very specific rules for the types of gifts given at particular times for particular events.

American gift customs are not as formal as in some other countries. Some people like to make the gifts they give. Other people like to buy gifts of a certain amount for some situations, or other people like to give money or gift certificates.

If someone close to you is celebrating a life event, it is appropriate to give them a gift or a card. If someone where you work is celebrating, co-workers often get together and sign one card or buy a present from the group with each person contributing a few dollars. Money is an acceptable gift for birthdays, graduations, and weddings. If you are in doubt about gifts or cards, ask a friend, co-worker or family member.

It is also common for the holidays in December (Christmas, Hanukkah, and Kwanzaa), to give a gift of money to people who provide personal services to you year-round. Some of these people include:

- ✦ Hair stylists and manicurists
- ✦ Mail delivery persons
- ✦ Newspaper delivery people
- ✦ Sanitation workers
- ✦ Any service people whom you know and work with on a regular basis.

Saying Thank You—There are two ways to say "thank you." You can verbally thank whoever gave you the gift. This is an expected and important custom. You may also want to send a written thank-you note to a person who has given you a gift. This is especially important for gifts given at the workplace or for formal occasions, such as a wedding or for the birth of a baby.

Vacationing in the United States

America offers many wonderful destinations and scenic natural beauty. There is much to see and do in America. If you have the opportunity to travel and see the country, you will find many different people and places. You can also learn about American history by traveling throughout the country. Americans generally get one to two weeks of vacation a year from work. The longer you work for a company, the more vacation time you may get.

There are many things to see and do in the United States.

Air Travel

Coast to coast, America covers a distance of approximately 3,000 miles or 5,000 km. If you were to drive without stopping from one coast to the other, it would take between five and seven days. In America, air travel is often the most common choice when trying to cover large distances between locations. It is the fastest way to travel.

Most people travel by air across the country.

Since the September 11, 2001, terrorist attacks on the World Trade Center in New York and the Pentagon in Washington, D.C., security at airports has greatly increased. In American airports, you will be required to provide proof of your identification with a picture ID. Airlines will typically ask for a driver's license or passport. You may be asked to show your picture identification several times during your travels. If you are traveling internationally, you will need your passport or visa.

Be sure to leave plenty of time to get through security checkpoints. Typically, you will want to arrive at the airport several hours in advance of your scheduled departure. You and your luggage may be inspected by security officials. Individual inspection of luggage is done at random.

Train Travel

Train travel is not as common as air travel in the United States. Most railroads are used to transport goods and supplies. Many parts of the country do not have passenger train service. The Northeast has more passenger train service than any other part of the country.

Bus Travel

Bus travel is an inexpensive way to travel across the country. Bus service is available in most towns and cities. The bus may make several stops along the route. Bus transportation can be less expensive than driving or flying.

Car Travel

If you want to really see America, travel by car. America has highways and interstates that will allow you to access any part of the country. Having a car allows you the freedom to go where you want, when you want. The main roads into the United States, called interstate roads, are geared to travel. You can find restaurants, gas stations and lodging at many road intersections.

Road Safety

Plan ahead when traveling in the United States. You should take a cellular phone with you. If you do not have a cellular phone, you should consider renting one for your trip. If you have an emergency anywhere in United States, dial 911 for the police. Keep your car doors locked, keep valuables in the trunk of the car, and do not give rides to people on the road.

Laws of the Road

While driving laws vary from state to state, here are some general rules to follow:

- The speed limit on the interstate highway varies from 55 mph to 75 mph
- All speeds are posted in mph (miles per hour) not kmp (kilometers per hour)
- Seat belts must be worn in all states
- All young children must be in car safety seats
- Check the Internet or library for rules you should know
- Do not drive while under the influence of alcohol

Young children must be in a car safety seat.

- Avoid using a cell phone while driving
- Safety on the road
    - Dial 911 for an emergency
    - Keep doors locked
    - Keep valuables in trunk
    - Do not pick up strangers
    - Plan ahead
    - Watch for "No Trespassing" signs.

Lodging

You have many lodging choices when traveling in the United States. You can choose from small budget motels to larger, more expensive hotels. Bed and Breakfast Inns are typically located in historical areas or small towns. Many hotels include a free continental breakfast in the price. Take your time and choose the best lodging for you.

You should be able to find lodging that fits your budget. You can usually get special rates, discounted rates, or promotional rates. Senior citizens (people 50 to 60 years of age and older) are often given a discount. Occasionally, a hotel will offer weekend specials or discount packages, especially during its less busy season.

Camping

America has many campgrounds located across the country. A **campground** is an area reserved for tents or recreational vehicles to stay for a short period of time. Most commercial campgrounds, like KOA, offer showers, laundry facilities, electrical hookups, pools, toilets, etc. If you are interested in camping, go to the bookstore or local library for a good camping guide. You will find thousands of campsites and a review of the quality of the campground.

The Convention and Visitors' Bureau

To get information about a specific destination, you may want to contact the Convention and Visitors' Bureau for that area. These offices have information about the sites to see, local places of interest, and the history of the area. To contact a Convention and Visitors' Bureau for a specific location, you can:

You can pick up travel brochures at rest stops and visitor centers.

- Look them up on the Internet
- Visit the reference area of the local library
- Call directory assistance for the bureau's phone number.

All state visitor centers will send you tourism information free of charge.

Local Library and Bookstores

Books are another great resource for information about places to travel. Hundreds of books are available that highlight different destinations around the country. Your local library or bookstores are filled with these types of books.

Eating Out

When traveling around the country, one thing you may notice is America has many **chain restaurants.** Chain restaurants are restaurants that go by the same name and serve similar food in cities all across the country. A chain restaurant menu stays the same from location to location. Some people feel the best food can be found in the small, local restaurants in a community, and not at a chain restaurant.

Travel with Identification

Whether you are traveling for a day or for a month, always carry identification with you. You may even want to carry your passport. Some places you may be asked to show identification are:

- At airports (airlines require identification with a photograph on it)
- At a hotel
- If you are renting a car.

Summary

In America, your work is only one part of your life. Taking care of your family, their health, security, and care is very important. To succeed in the workplace, you must be able to succeed at home. If you understand the medical system, child-care options, and ways to be secure, you can make wise decisions. Learn about the holidays and customs of America. Take time to travel and see what a diverse and beautiful country this is.

Glossary

Assisted-living facility: a hotel-type setting attached to, or near, a care facility, where an elderly person can live independently with some daily or weekly assistance as needed.

Campground is an area reserved for tents or recreational vehicles to stay for a short period of time.

Chain restaurants: restaurants that go by the same name and serve similar food in cities all across the country.

Clinic: a medical office with a group of doctors.

Co-pay: a portion of the bill you need to pay when visiting the doctor or buying medicine.

Day care: a company licensed to watch children.

Emergency medical team (EMT): staff an ambulance that answers calls for health emergencies.

Emergency room (ER): area of a hospital equipped to care for people with serious and immediate health needs.

Extended family: a family that has parents, grandparents, aunts, uncles, brothers, sisters, and children all living in the same, or in nearby, homes. Not common in the United States.

Fire department: the local government department responsible for preventing and putting out fires.

Gangs: groups of people (usually youths) who stake out territory and rights in an area.

General practitioner: a doctor who has general knowledge of medicine and can give care for the most common illnesses.

Gerontologist: a doctor specializing in the health of the elderly.

Immunization: an injection of medication that helps the body protect itself from diseases.

Internist: a doctor specializing in the treatment of internal organs.

Nursing home: a facility that provides living arrangements and care for the elderly, chronically ill, or individuals recovering from surgery or injuries.

Ophthalmologists: professionals licensed to do eye surgery in addition to standard eye exams and care.

Optometrists: professionals licensed to do eye exams and prescribe eyeglasses and contact lenses.

Oral surgeons: usually have special equipment and facilities for surgical dental procedures.

Otolaryngologist/ENT: a doctor specializing in problems with the ear, nose, and throat.

Outpatient surgery: a surgery, after which you go home, rather than remaining in the hospital.

Over-the-counter drugs: medicines you can purchase without a doctor's prescription.

Pediatrician: a doctor specializing in children's health.

Podiatrist: a doctor specializing in foot problems.

Police department: local government department responsible for maintaining order, enforcing laws, and preventing and detecting crime.

Pre-approved/Pre-admitted: a non-emergency surgery or hospital stay for which you or your doctor have obtained approval from your insurance company.

Preschool: a school-style day care for children typically between the ages of 3 and 6.

Prescription drugs: medicines your doctor will tell you to take for specific medical conditions.

Retirement home or community: a housing complex where an elderly person who has retired from their life's work may choose to live. Some retirement homes offer on-site nursing as well.

Senior citizens: generally people 60 years of age and older.

Senior day-care center: a facility with trained staff that assists the elderly or disabled in participation in daily activities outside their home.

Specialist: a doctor who has had additional training in a particular area of medicine.

Surgery: a medical procedure done by a doctor to treat an injury or disease.

Exercises

1. Internet Exercise (see Pages 211-212 for more information on the Internet): Log on to any search engine (www.google.com, www.dogpile.com,

www.yahoo.com) and search by the following terms to learn more about balancing your home and work life. For many of these, you may choose to put the name of the city or state you live in before the word or phrase. Doing this will bring up local information as well as national information.

- Childcare
- Elder care
- Immediate care centers
- Doctors
- Dentists
- Optometrists
- Required immunizations
- Over-the-counter drugs
- How to feel safe
- American Automobile Association (AAA)
- Traffic accidents
- National holidays
- Holidays
- American vacation destinations
- Federal Aviation Administration (FAA)
- Road safety
- KOA
- Hotel Motel Associations
- Convention and Visitor's Bureau

2. Time to plan a vacation! Get an atlas or road map and plan a trip you would like to take. You will need to determine where you will go and what you will do there, how you will get there, how much time it will take, what it will cost, and anything else you may need to know for a successful trip. You can research this on the Internet or at your local library. Should you be feeling adventurous, take the trip and see something new. America has a lot to see!

Chapter 12

Education

Education is important in America. In many cases, a specific level of education may be required to get hired for a job. Many employers want to hire a person with at least a basic high school education. After completing high school, many people choose to go on to learn new skills or train for a new profession. This chapter takes a look at the different choices we have for education in the United States, from childhood to adulthood and beyond.

Expanding Your Education

Many people come to America specifically for their education. Higher education can help you:

- Secure a higher paying job
- Advance your career
- Have a feeling of self-fulfillment.

You need to ask yourself some questions:

- What type of education do I need to get a good job and to advance in my career?
- Will my employer or new school recognize my education from my home country?
- Can I work full-time and still go to school?

In This Chapter

- Continuing your education in America
- Education options in addition to college
- Children's education
- College and advanced education

Transferring Your Education from Home

If you are planning on attending a college or university in America, you should ask if you can get credit for the courses you have taken in your home country. Colleges and universities require official transcripts. A **transcript** is a list of the courses you have taken and the grade you received with your school's stamp. If you have graduated from another school, bring your diploma or degree and a copy of the school's class catalog (a book with a description of each class). If your school has been accredited, bring information about the accreditation standards. **Accreditation** is certification by an official organization that the school has met certain set standards. Be sure to have the address of the school and a contact that can verify your information.

Professional Certifications

Many people want to expand their skills without having to attend school for several years. To do this, a professional certification can help you. **Certification** is extra training that will provide you with expertise in a specified area. Once you have completed the training or classes, you will receive a certificate to show you have skills in this area.

Certification can be completed in much less time than a college or university degree. Depending on the type of training you need, you may wish to take a group of classes, a week-long seminar, or a single day of training. Many employers will pay for training related to your job. Training can be a great way to expand your skills and advance in your career.

Individual Classes

Local high schools or colleges may offer **continuing education classes**. These classes are designed for adults to teach very specific skills to adults. For example, if you wanted to improve your typing skills, you could take a class to study typing; or if you wanted to learn about a certain software product you could also take a class for that software. Taking these classes could also help you improve your English skills. Many continuing education programs also offer English as a Second Language (ESL) classes to help people new to America improve their English language skills.

Immigrant Views

"Get an education to compete in the job market. Be ready to do any kind of work till you achieve your career goal."

Hardial Deol, immigrated from India in the early 1970's

Seminars and Workshops

Another way to learn specific skills is to attend seminars and workshops in your area. Many companies offer half-day, or one-day professional seminars and workshops on a variety of topics. Topics can range from "Improving Your Communication Skills" to "Time Management." There is typically a charge for these classes. The seminars are usually held at a local hotel or business. If you want to attend one of these seminars, you need to register with the company providing it. You should expect to pay for the seminar before attending it.

The American Education System

Children in the United States are guaranteed a free public education by the government. Children are required to attend school from ages 6 to 16. Each state has a board of education that regulates its schools. Standards and requirements differ among states.

Public education is available to all children.

The quality of the education can also be different among school systems. Many Americans examine the quality of local schools before choosing a place to live or accepting a job in a certain community. A good school system will increase the value of homes and property in the area.

Public vs. Private Schools

Private schools offer another option to education. Public schools are free to all children, where private schools are more exclusive and charge money for their services. Some examples of private schools include:

- Parochial schools, schools supported by a church. These schools offer standard education, with a special education in religion. They support the values of the sponsoring church.
- Montessori schools offer more independent and individualized learning. Montessori schools generally are available for children from preschool through middle school.
- Boarding schools, where the child goes to live at the school, are available but are uncommon in the United States.

Grades and Grade Levels

In the American school system, children are tracked by grade level. Students are tested on all subjects and receive grades on their work. The grading scale will vary by school district, but is generally broken down like this:

Grade	Work is...
A	Excellent
B	Above Average
C	Average
D	Below Average
F	Failing

If a student receives a failing grade, they may be held back. Students who are held back must repeat the grade they fail. Schools are required to offer assistance to students performing below their grade level. Many schools also offer gifted and talented classes that give more challenging work for advanced students.

This chart lists common levels of schools available and the grades that attend each school. These grades can vary from area to area.

School	Average Age	Features
Preschool (optional)	3-4	Preparation for school, learning numbers, letters, social skills.
Kindergarten (optional in some states)	5-6	Preparation for school, learning numbers, letters, social skills, beginning reading.
Elementary Grades 1-4	6-9	Focus on reading, mathematics, writing, basic knowledge – students have one teacher for most subjects.
Middle School Grades 5-6	10-11	Sometimes combined into elementary school, same focus as elementary with more independence, different teachers for some subjects.

School	Average Age	Features
Junior High Grades 7-8	12-13	More independence, begin to have some choices in subjects taken.
Senior High 9th - Freshman 10th - Sophomore 11th - Junior 12th - Senior	14-18	Flexible schedules, some required subjects, more choices on special subjects. Preparation for college or work. High school diploma received upon graduation.

GED—High School Equivalent

In America, people are expected to earn a high school diploma before going to college. If you do not have the equivalent of a high school from your home country, you can earn a **GED— General Equivalency Diploma**.

GED classes are usually offered during nights and on weekends. Check with your local school system. They will tell you how to enroll. Many schools also offer multi-lingual assistance.

It is important in the American workplace to have at least a high school diploma or GED. This documents your ability to do basic reading, math, problem solving, and communications. Before hiring someone, most companies will require a high school diploma, GED, or equivalent. All universities and colleges require a high school diploma or GED for you to enroll.

Advanced Education

Bachelor's Degree

Most colleges and universities in the United States offer two-year and four-year programs. **Junior colleges** generally offer two-year programs. In a two-year program, you can take basic subjects and then transfer your coursework to a four-year program at a larger university. Many colleges also offer certificates and short-term classes.

Most universities also offer a Bachelor of Science or Bachelor of Arts degree. Bachelor's degrees are also called four-year degrees. A full-time student can complete a degree in four years. When looking to enroll in a degree program, consider the following things:

+ Some programs require you to be a full-time student for a specific number of terms
+ "Senior projects" may be required in addition to specific course work
+ You are often required to take additional courses in general studies outside your major
+ If your high school degree or equivalent is from a country other than the United States, you may be asked to pass an English equivalency exam
+ High school transcripts and SAT scores are usually required
+ Some degrees require internships for completion

Diplomas and certifications show your experience.

Keep in mind after you earn a degree, you may still need to pass a professional exam. Teaching, accounting, and nursing are just a few professions requiring a professional exam. Not all professional exams are accepted in every state. Each state may have different requirements.

Associate Degree

In America, many colleges and universities offer associate degrees, or two-year degrees. Associate degrees often give you the training necessary to begin work. Many people obtain an associate degree to get a job, and then build on the degree for a four-year degree. Four-year degrees are called bachelor's degrees.

It is important to understand your program's requirements. Do not be surprised if you are asked to take courses not directly related to your interest. Be sure to ask questions about the schedule of courses. Usually, full-time students who take four to five classes a term can finish an associates degree in two years.

Some classes may only be available once a year or less. Save the course catalog from the year you enroll. It will determine the courses required to complete your degree. Colleges and universities often change requirements from year to year.

Technical Colleges

Many cities across the United States have **technical or vocational schools**. These are places where you go to learn skills and train for a specific job. An example of this is a culinary school, where you go to study how to be a chef. This is a great place to start if you want to learn new skills, but you are not ready to go to a university to earn a degree.

Summary

The American government guarantees a free public education. Regardless of your background, education, or history, you may choose to achieve further education. America offers many choices for continuing your education and improving your skills. The more knowledge you have to offer, the more valuable you become to a company. The more valuable you are, the better your chances are of advancing in your career and being paid a higher amount!

Becoming successful and having the ability to be independent are two goals most Americans strive for. America allows you to choose how you wish to pursue success and independence.

Glossary

Accredited: a school approved or certified by an official organization.

Associate degree: a two-year degree offered by many colleges and universities that provides you with the training necessary to begin work.

Bachelor's degree: a four-year degree from a college or university.

Certification: extra training that will provide you with expertise in a specified area.

Continuing education classes: classes designed to teach very specific things to adults, such as English as a Second Language (ESL), typing skills, or how to use a specific software program.

General Equivalency Diploma (GED): a certificate documenting your ability to do basic reading, math, problem solving, and communications at the level of a high school graduate.

Junior college: a college offering a two-year program where the coursework can then be transferred to a college or university offering a four-year program.

Technical/vocational schools: schools that teach skills and provide training for a specific job.

Transcript: a list of the courses you have taken and the grade you received in other schools.

Exercises

1. Internet Exercise (see Pages 209-210 for more information on the Internet): Log on to any search engine (www.google.com, www.dogpile.com, www.yahoo.com) and search by the following terms to learn more about educational options America has to offer:

    - Transferring educational credits
    - Professional certifications
    - American education
    - Private education
    - American public school systems
    - Getting a GED
    - Colleges and universities
    - Technical schooling
    - Higher education.

2. What do you want to be when you grow up? Many careers encourage you to do more than just get a college degree. Many jobs will even require you to get a professional certification. Research the career you want to pursue and see if there are any professional certifications you can work on now or you can plan to work on after college.

Chapter 13

Getting a Job and Keeping a Job

One of the fastest ways to gain independence in America is by getting a job. You will have many different choices. It is important to find a job that fits what you do best and allows you to make the amount of money you want.

Before You Start Looking for a Job

Start by making a list of the skills you have or the things you do well. Be sure to include any talents and abilities you have. You will also want to add things you did in your country before coming to America. Finally, make a list of the skills you do not have but want to learn.

Use these lists when you look for a job. Try to match the skills you have with the jobs you will be applying for. If you do not speak English, your choices may be limited. Do not give up. Learn the language and keep trying to improve your employment situation.

Sometimes the job you accept may not be exactly the one you want. Most jobs will allow you to advance to higher levels. In order to advance, you will have to work hard and be willing to learn new things.

In This Chapter

- Ways to find a job
- Applying for a job
- What to expect in an interview
- Resumés and portfolios
- Understanding job salary and benefits
- Success in the workplace
- Diversity and culture in the American workplace

Finding Job Openings

You are now ready to start looking! The first step is finding out what jobs are available. Be sure to look in several places. Many businesses will advertise in one place and not in another. You may get one job lead from the newspaper and a second one from the Internet! Let us talk about some of the places you can look to see where companies are hiring.

Network with Your Friends

When looking for a job, a good place to start is with your friends and mentors. They may know about good places to work. Keep in mind, the jobs they may know about may not be advertised, but because they suggested you, you may get a great job!

Newspapers

Read the want ads in the classified section of the local newspaper. Many employers place help wanted ads in the Sunday newspaper. Some newspapers have an entire section of the Sunday edition just for employment ads. Ads are organized by job type. Usually, the types of jobs can include:

- Professional
- Technical
- Clerical
- Service
- Sales
- Medical
- Trade.

Most newspaper ads indicate the position, some responsibilities or requirements needed for the job, and how to contact the employer.

Use the want ads to find local jobs.

Help Wanted Signs

Many companies will place signs in the window when they are hiring. In this case, you need to go to the front desk and ask for an application.

Walk In and Ask

You may be interested in working for a particular company. It is acceptable to go in and ask if they are accepting applications or have any positions open. Many companies will take your information and see if they have anything open that meets your skills.

Local Radio Stations, Cable TV, and Fliers

Some employers will advertise job openings at the end of an advertisement for their company on the radio or on TV. Many local cable TV stations also have a program where they list job openings at a certain time of the day or week. You can also find job postings listed on bulletin boards in grocery stores.

Look for help wanted signs in local shops.

The Internet

Another common way to find a job is to post your resumé or qualifications on the Internet. There are many job hosting sites available. You can also find job boards for specific fields of expertise. Employers who are interested in you will send you an e-mail or contact you to set up an interview. It is becoming increasingly more popular for employers to do phone interviews before a contact interview to screen applicants.

Hiring Agencies

Hiring agencies are companies that specialize in placing people in jobs. Should you choose to use the services of a hiring agency, you will need to register with the agency. The agency will contact potential employers to set up interviews. If you are hired, the company pays a fee to the agency. Do not sign up with a firm that requires you to pay a fee.

Immigrant Views

If you could do it again, what would you do differently?

"Keeping an open mind to changes and challenges. I would welcome any opportunity coming my way from any industry that recognizes my skills and talents."

Prakash Naik immigrated from Bangalore, India in 1999.

Preparing for the Job Application Process

Some companies will let you take the application home to fill it out. However, most companies will not let you take the application with you. It is a good idea to have everything with you that you will need to fill out the application. Most applications will ask you to list any jobs you have had, the employers you have worked for, and the dates of your employment. You will also want to list any awards or honors you may have received.

Documentation

Make sure you have all your documents together to prove you are eligible to work. This includes your:

- Passport and work visa
- Alien Card
- Social security number
- Driver's license.

References

You should bring a list of two to four references to the interview. A **reference** is a person you know who is willing to talk to employers about you and your work experience. There are two types of references an employer may be interested in speaking to:

- A **professional reference** is usually someone who can talk about your work experience and professionalism
- A **personal reference** is a friend or mentor who can tell the employer about you.

Be sure to include the name, address, and phone number for each reference. Indicate whether they are a personal or professional reference.

Work Samples

Some employers may ask to see samples of your work. Put together a binder or portfolio containing samples of your work and experiences. A portfolio can help you stand out and be remembered by employers. This is especially true when you are applying for a job where there is a lot of competition for the position.

Getting Ready for the Interview

There are many things you can do to make a good impression during your interview. Some things you should remember to do can include:

+ Being well rested
+ Being clean and well-groomed
+ Wearing clothes that are neat and clean.

The type of clothing you wear to an interview will depend on the job you are applying for. If you will be working in an office, wear more formal clothing, even if the other people are wearing casual clothes. The clothes you wear will tell the interviewer a lot about you.

Questions

In most interviews, not only will the employer ask you questions, the person conducting the interview will expect questions from you. Before the interview, make a list of questions to ask the interviewer. These questions can be about the job, the company, the area of the city, or transportation. Asking questions shows the interviewer you have prepared for the interview and are interested in the company and the job.

Filling Out a Job Application

Read the entire application. Fill out everything and print neatly. Do not leave blank spaces. If you do not understand something, do not be afraid to ask! People are usually very happy to help you. Keep your application neat. Try to avoid erasing or crossing out information. **Make sure you sign the form**. Not signing the application is a common mistake that people make.

+ Read entire application
+ Fill out every line
+ Ask if you do not understand
+ Be neat
+ Sign the application form.

Ask if you need help filling out an application.

Resumés

A **resumé** is a formal listing of your job experiences and education. In some countries this is called a curriculum vitae. The resumé is a standard tool used in the United States to get a job. When answering a job ad, send a resumé to the employer along with a **cover letter**. A cover letter is a letter expressing interest in the job and briefly explaining any qualifications.

The design of your resumé, and the information included in it, may be different depending on the position you want. Most resumés contain the following information:

- A short sentence about the kind of position you want and what skills you can offer the employer.
- A list of your work history. Include job title, employer, dates of employment, and your job responsibilities for each job. If you have had many jobs, list the ones most similar to the current job.
- List your education. You may include high school, colleges, and universities attended, or certificates and training you have received. Include the name and location of the schools you attended, the dates of your attendance, the degrees received, your areas of study, and any special education you received.
- If you have received any awards or honors, you can include these in a separate section of the resumé.
- List or describe any special skills you have. These skills can include the different languages you speak, read, or write.
- Include your name, address, and a phone number where they can contact you. It is also common to include an e-mail address, if you have one.

There are many books on creating a resumé. Look in the career section of a bookstore or library, or use the Internet to find more information on resumés.

Interviewing for a Job

Starting the Interview

It is time for the interview! Be five to 10 minutes early for the interview. Whatever you do, do not be late. Try not to be nervous, just be yourself. SMILE!

When you greet the interviewer, shake hands with him or her and smile. Introduce yourself so they know how to pronounce your name correctly.

During the Interview

Make eye contact with the interviewer on a regular basis. Eye contact is very important in an interview. It shows you are interested in the job and helps the interviewer trust you. Listen carefully and completely to any questions you are asked before answering them. Answer questions truthfully and completely. Be confident in yourself, but do not be overconfident. Do not brag about your accomplishments, but be modest and truthful.

Be professional.

Ending the Interview

Wait until the end of the interview to ask any questions you have. The interviewer will typically ask you if you have any questions for him or her. Once the interview is over, thank the interviewer for their time. Shake his or her hand and smile!

When you go home, write a thank-you note to the interviewer. Thank them for taking the time to interview you. Keep the note simple and professional. Make sure you spell the person's name correctly. Send the note within 48 hours of the interview.

Wages/Benefits

Once you have found a job you like, you will want to consider:

- How much it pays
- Whether it is an hourly or salary position
- Whether it is part-time or full-time
- What type of benefits the company offers.

Salary vs. Hourly—What Is the Difference?

Hourly employees get paid for each hour and minute they work. An hourly rate is agreed upon before you are hired. The time you work is recorded on a time card or in a computer. A **salaried employee** is paid a fixed rate for each pay period. Salaried employees are typically offered a specific amount of money on an annual basis.

Pay Periods

Different jobs have different payment methods. When you are hired, you will be told how you will be paid. If you are paid hourly, ask how many hours there will be in a workweek. You can then calculate what your weekly paycheck may be. If you are salaried, you can divide your annual salary, after taxes, by the number of pay periods you have in the year to calculate what your weekly paycheck may be.

Work Hours

A **part-time** employee usually works less than 35 hours a week. **Full-time** employees work up to 40 hours a week and may work overtime. **Overtime** is hours worked more than regularly scheduled hours (typically more than 40 hours a week). If you are in an **employee pool**, you will work when you are called. **Seasonal workers** are typically used only during the season they are needed. Lifeguarding during the summer, the Christmas season sales help, harvest time, and snow plowing are all examples of seasonal employment.

Benefits

Benefits can include insurance, paid time off, holidays, money for retirement accounts, uniforms, some combination of these, or more. Employers usually offer benefits only to full-time employees. When you are looking for a job you may want to ask for an explanation of the benefits. Chapter 14 gives a full explanation of what benefits are and how they work.

You Got the Job; Workplace Guidelines

All the hard work has paid off. You have been offered the job you wanted. Now what? Your new boss will tell you when and where to report to work.

On your first day of work be sure to bring your identification and paperwork. You will be asked to fill out tax information and will need your passport and visa, your social security card and alien card.

You will probably be filling out a lot of paperwork for the company. The paperwork will help the

Things to Bring on your First Day

company to process your salary and benefits. If you have any questions while completing the paperwork, just ask.

How to Act on Your First Day

Dress appropriately. Make sure your clothes are neat and clean. Be sure you are clean and well-groomed.

Do not be afraid to ask questions. Most employers begin by giving you a company orientation. An **orientation** is when they tell you about their company and their policies. You may have a co-worker assigned to you to help you meet people and show you around.

Be friendly and smile. Try not to be shy. Introduce yourself to people you do not know. You do not have to wait for people to introduce themselves to you. If you introduce yourself first, you will be seen as a friendly person.

Hints on Time!

Be sure to be on time.

Remember in a previous chapter when we talked about the importance of time and timeliness in America? It is critical you are on time every day for work. Everything you do will eventually affect the decision to give you a raise or a promotion. **Start on time**—In the United States, this means you are there, ready to work, at least 10 minutes early. If it takes you some extra time to put your personal belongings away—plan for that time.

Breaks—Breaks are limited to a specific amount of time. If you have 15 minutes for your break, that includes the time it takes you to get from and to your workstation.

Lunch Hour—The time rules for breaks are also true of your lunch hour. You need to plan for drive time or walking time. If you have an hour for lunch, you should be back 60 minutes from the time your lunch break started.

Working overtime—You may be asked to work late, or **overtime**. If you work an additional four-hour period in a day, you are legally entitled to another break. Ask your employer how extra breaks are handled.

Coming in late—What happens when you are late for work? First you need to call your employer as soon as you know you are going to be late. Keep your supervisor's number with you. Let your supervisor know when you expect to be in. Try to reach a person. If you cannot reach a person, leave a message. Lateness is looked upon negatively in America.

Calling In or Not Coming to Work

If you are ill or cannot come to work, you must let your supervisor know. Many companies require you to call in at least two hours before your start time. Many companies have specific policies on absenteeism. Be sure to completely read your employee handbook. If you call in sick, your employer may ask for a note from the doctor stating you were ill.

Finding a substitute—Your job may allow you to not come in to work if you find someone to work your shift. Be sure the person is qualified, currently works for the company, and has performed your job before. Make sure you tell your supervisor. Be careful, and be sure you ask someone you trust to cover your shift. If the person you have chosen does not come in, it will be your responsibility.

Attitude

Your attitude may also determine how people value your work. Be pleasant and always tell the truth. Speak in a professional way. Do not nag or gossip about other employees. Enjoy your job. Many employers see your attitude as a crucial part of your job.

Training

Being open-minded and willing to learn can be very important to your success. Employers will invest money to train you. They may send you to classes to learn more about your job. You might learn how to improve your speaking, learn more about technology, or how to be a leader. Training is a costly investment your company chooses to make in you. Take advantage of those opportunities.

Company Culture

To be successful in a company and to advance, it is important to understand the company's culture. **Company culture** is:

- What a company believes in
- Its values
- Its focus

✦ The behaviors it expects and supports.

It is important to note company cultures are as diverse as America. There is no standard for company culture. Corporate cultures may be less or more formal.

You may have problems adjusting to the company's work environment. Knowing and understanding the culture will help you adjust more quickly. It can also help you become more effective at your job.

Understanding Diversity in the American Workplace

There are several practices or "norms" in the American workplace you may not have in the country you came from.

Cultural Differences

In America, there are many different races, cultural backgrounds, and ethnicities. It would not be uncommon to work with people who have different color skin, features, clothing, etc. It is important to try to learn about and to respect the differences. In America, a person's age is typically seen as unimportant. In some cultures, age is more respected than in America. In America, it is not unusual for someone who is 60 to be working for a supervisor who is 28. It is important for you to understand that regardless of age, your manager must still be respected as your supervisor. It is also becoming standard for workers to retire later in life than ever before.

Religious Values

Religion in America is very diverse. Various religions have very different practices and traditions. Do not assume your manager understands the needs of your religion. If you have special needs or accommodations because of your religious beliefs, it is important you communicate them to your manager. If you choose not to communicate them to your manager, do not expect him or her to be able to provide for you.

Women in the Workplace

Women make up a large part of the working population in America. Do not be surprised if you have a woman who is your boss. This may be very different from what you are used to. You will need to treat your female bosses and co-workers the same way you would treat male ones!

Personal Values

Sometimes you will be in an environment you are not familiar with. You may not agree with everything you find in your workplace. You may even find that while you are being open to new things, others are not. You should have a plan in mind for how you want to deal with these situations. Have a mentor or friend help you make this plan. It is important to try to teach those who are ignorant about your culture, what it is that you are all about.

Company Policies

Most companies have company policies, best practices, procedures. These policies may include things like:

- Equal Employment Opportunity policy
- Nondiscrimination policy
- Harassment policies
- Drug and alcohol policies.

Other policies may be more specific to the jobs. Some of these may include:

- Attendance policy
- Call-Off policy
- Personal business policies.

Make sure you take the time to learn the policies. In order to be successful with a company, it is important you follow all policies and procedures that are in place.

Smoking

Smoking is usually not permitted in the work environment. Many people find it offensive and undesirable. There is usually a designated place where you can go to smoke. Smoking in an area where you are not supposed to smoke can be a very serious offense and may result in your losing your job. Be sure to follow any smoking policies your company may have in place.

Summary

When you are looking for a job, be sure to research not only the job, but the company as well. Use everything you can, including the newspaper, radio, and Internet, to help you do your research. Ask your friends and mentor questions and listen carefully to their answers.

Whether you are trying to get a job or have a job already, it is important to always act professionally. Treat everyone with respect and keep a positive attitude. In order to be seen as being professional, you will want to show up on time, be ready to work, learn the company culture, and follow the policies and rules. Finally, take advantage of every training opportunity and learn whatever you can. Take any classes the company offers and plan for your next position!

Glossary

Company culture: what a company believes in, its values, its focus, and the behaviors it expects and supports.

Cover letter: a letter expressing interest in a job and briefly explaining any qualifications.

Employee pool: you will work when you are called.

Full-time: employees work up to 40 hours a week, and may work overtime.

Hiring agencies: companies that specialize in placing people in jobs.

Hourly employee: an employee who is paid for each hour and minute they work according to an agreed-upon hourly rate.

Orientation: is when they tell you about their company and their policies.

Overtime: hours worked more than regular schedule hours (typically more than 40 hours a week).

Part-time: employee usually works less than 35 hours a week.

Reference: a person you know who is willing to talk to employers about you and your work experience. A professional reference is usually someone who can talk about your work experience and professionalism. A personal reference is a friend or mentor who can tell the employer about you.

Resumé: a formal listing of your job experiences and education. In some countries this is called a curriculum vitae.

Salaried employee: an employee who is paid a fixed rate for each pay period no matter how many hours they work during that period.

Seasonal workers: typically used only during the season they are needed.

Exercises

1. Internet Exercise (see Pages 209-210 for more information on the Internet): Log on to any search engine (www.google.com, www.dogpile.com, www.yahoo.com) and search by the following terms to learn more about finding and getting a job. For many of these, you may choose to put the

name of the city or state you live in before the word or phrase. Doing this will bring up local information as well as national information.

- Finding a job
- Careers
- Job classifieds
- Headhunters
- Immigrant documentation for jobs
- How to write a resumé
- Writing a cover letter
- Career portfolios
- Learnovation
- Interviewing techniques
- Salary and benefits
- Workplace etiquette
- Corporate culture.

2. Everyone has a resumé; it is time to set yourself apart! Start creating your career portfolio now. A career portfolio can include your:

- Personal philosophy
- Professional goals
- Resumé
- Work samples
- Community service
- Professional memberships
- Professional certifications
- References.

Start now saving samples of your best work. Get a file box and collect any samples you may have now. If you do not have any, spend time working on your work philosophy and goals.

Chapter 14

Taxes and On-the-Job Benefits

If you work or live in the United States, you will help to support the government by paying taxes. **Taxes** are extra fees charged on goods and property you buy and the money you earn. Much of these taxes come back to us as government services and the care of our communities. For example, road repair is paid for with state taxes. The **Internal Revenue Service (IRS)** is the government agency in charge of the collection of taxes.

America does not have socialized medicine. You pay for your own health care. In America, many employers offer benefits. **Benefits** are extra services or features besides money that an employer offers to employees. Benefits often include some form of a health care plan. In some cases, benefits are completely paid for by the company. Other times, the cost of the benefit is split between the employer and the employee.

By providing benefits, employers can get good employees to work for them. Some of the common benefits companies provide include:

+ Health insurance
+ Life insurance
+ Vision insurance
+ Saving or pension plans
+ 401(k) plans (retirement plans)
+ Paid time off.

In This Chapter
+ Paying taxes on the money you earn
+ How employment benefits work
+ Health benefits
+ Savings benefits
+ Other benefits

Taxes

Everyone who earns money must pay taxes to the federal government. Most states also have a tax on your income. You fill out tax forms when you begin a job. The government will take out a certain portion of each paycheck automatically. In January, your employer will give you a **W-2 statement**, that lists how much you earned in the previous year and how much tax you paid. You must submit a tax form to the government before April 15. This form shows what you have earned and what taxes you have already paid. If you have paid more than the government requires, you will get a check back. If you need to pay more taxes, you must write a check to cover the amount due.

Tax forms are available at the post office, the public library, and on the federal government's website (www.irs.gov). Accountants and companies with tax services can assist you in preparing your taxes. These groups usually charge a fee. It is not uncommon to pay anywhere from $50 to $200 for your tax forms to be prepared.

Types of Taxes

There are several types of taxes you must pay:

- **Federal income tax**—you pay a percentage of your income based upon tax law.
- **State income tax**—many states also require you to pay taxes on the money you earn.
- **Local income tax**—may also be required depending on the local tax laws.
- **FICA**—7.5% of your paycheck goes to the Social Security office. Your employer matches that amount. This money comes out of your paycheck each time you are paid. You can request a summary of your social security account from the Social Security office.
- **Self-Employment tax**—If you are self-employed, you pay a self-employment tax of 15%.

Many Americans find it confusing to complete taxes. Ask a friend or mentor for help completing your taxes. If you do not file a tax return, you may have to pay more money later, or the government may take part of your check to pay taxes owed. You may also have paid too much money to the government and may need to get it back!

How Do Benefits Work?

There are three types of benefits employers can provide. These include:

- **Health benefits**—Health benefits will help prepare you financially for unexpected health-related events as well as assist with the payment of regular health checkups. For example, if you have health insurance and become ill or injured, you will only have to pay a portion of the bill. The insurance company will pay most of your medical bill.
- **Savings plan**—A 401(k), or savings plan, is a financial investment for retirement. In other words, for every dollar you put in, the company matches it with an agreed-upon amount.
- **Extra features**—Paid time off or a company issued automobile is a **perk** of the job, or something extra you get other than your base salary. A bonus plan is another type of a perk.

It is important to understand how benefits work and how you can use them to save you money. You can refuse any benefits offered to you. For example, if you do not have the need for glasses or contacts, you can refuse vision insurance and save money.

When Do You Pay for Benefits?

The cost of any benefits you choose to accept is taken directly out of your paycheck before you receive it. The amounts you were charged for your benefits will be printed on your paycheck "stub."

Many companies offer "direct deposit" as an employee benefit. **Direct deposit** is when your company deposits your paycheck into your personal checking or savings account. You do not have to go to the bank and deposit or cash your check, and the money is immediately available on payday. There is no cost to you to use this benefit. If you use automatic deposit, you will still receive a copy of your paycheck with your tax and benefit information on the stub.

Pretax Option

Many employers offer their employees a **Pretax option**. This means when your benefits are automatically taken out of your paycheck, they are taken out before taxes are calculated on your income. Taxes are figured on the amount of your paycheck left after benefits have been taken out. This option can save you tax money.

Health Benefits

Life Insurance

Life insurance is an benefit you may choose to carry that will pay your **beneficiaries** (the people you choose to receive the money) when you die. The most popular type of life insurance to carry is term life insurance. **Term life insurance** will only be paid to your beneficiaries if you die while you are paying the policy premiums. There are other types of life insurance that include investment and loan options. Study the details of life insurance options carefully and choose what is best for you.

Health Insurance

Americans must pay for their doctor's visits and prescription medicine. The cost can be very expensive. Health insurance will help with this expense. Many employers will purchase group medical coverage or insurance and offer it as a benefit. This allows you to have insurance at a lower cost than if you bought it yourself. The employer usually pays a portion of the premium cost. You will pay the remainder.

There are different types of coverage and coverage options. When selecting your preferred coverage, you need to be familiar with these terms:

Co-pay—The portion of the cost of a doctor's visit you have to pay. This amount is determined by your insurance company. The remainder of the cost of the visit is covered by your health insurance.

PPO—Preferred Provider Organization. A PPO allows you to choose a doctor from an approved listing of doctors provided by your insurance company. As long as you visit doctors on the list provided, you will only be responsible for a small portion of the payment. If you choose to go to a doctor not on the list, you will be responsible for a larger portion, or the entire cost of the visit.

HMO—Health Maintenance Organization. An HMO is a group of doctors that join together to form an organization. Typically, HMOs are usually associated with specific hospitals. You can only visit the doctors associated with the HMO. Should you choose to see a doctor not associated with the HMO, you will not be covered by your insurance.

Referral—A referral is when a doctor recommends you visit another doctor, typically a specialist. A referral is needed in order for your insurance to pay for a visit.

Deductible—A predetermined amount of money you pay before your insurance coverage will begin payment. For example, suppose you broke your arm and the hospital charged you $600 for your care. If you had a $200 deductible, you would pay $200 before your insurance company would pay for the rest of your bill. Some of the common amounts include $100, $500, $1,000, and $2,000. The lower your deductible, the more expensive your insurance plan will be.

Prescription Drug Card—Some insurance policies will cover the cost of prescription drugs. Your insurance company will issue you a prescription drug card if your policy covers prescription drugs. You need to select a pharmacy that accepts your policy's prescription drug plan. Present the card at a pharmacy and your medication will be given to you at a greatly reduced cost.

Generic Drugs—Generic drugs are drugs that do not have a brand name. An example brand-name drug would be Tylenol. The generic drug for Tylenol is acetaminophen. Generic drugs contain the same active ingredients as the brand-name drugs, but are less expensive. Often the packaging and appearance of the drugs are different as well.

Vision Coverage

Vision plans are an optional benefit you can choose to refuse. Vision plans provide coverage for eye exams, glasses, and contact lenses. Many vision plans will only pay for either one pair of glasses or contact lenses each year. If you have no history of vision problems, you may choose to decline vision coverage.

Dental Coverage

Dental coverage is similar to medical insurance. Some dental plans allow you to go to any dentist. Other dental plans require you to choose a dentist from a list provided by the insurance company. Your coverage may or may not have a deductible or a co-pay. Most dental plans fully cover the cost of routine checkups and cleaning with the exception of a small co-pay. Service coverages will vary from plan to plan. Ask your employer for the specific details about your dental plan.

Elective Insurance

Many companies offer voluntary, or elective, insurance plans. Typically, employers do not pay any portion of elective insurance plans. Some elective insurance plans can include voluntary life insurance, cancer assistance insurance, short-term disability and long-term disability.

> **A Word from Kooner...** Take advantage of the benefits you are offered on the job. It may seem like you are losing money from your paycheck by paying for life or health insurance, but if you need to go to the doctor or have an emergency, treatment can be very expensive. Insurance is the way most people pay for health care in America.

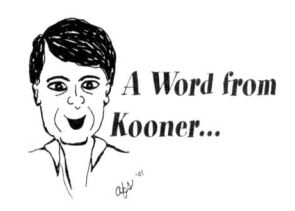

Savings and Investment Benefits

401(K) Savings Plans

A 401(k) saving plan is a great way to save money for your retirement. These plans are pretax programs. Many employers offer some form of a 401(k) plan. Some employers will also match a portion of the money you put into your plan. For example, for every dollar you contribute, your company may contribute an additional 25 cents to your plan.

Many companies that match contributions to your 401(k) plan will have a vesting schedule. A **vesting schedule** requires you to work for the company for a certain number of years before you can use the money the company has contributed to your plan.

In a vesting schedule, for every year you work with a company you earn a percentage of the money the company added to your account. At some point you will be 100% vested and all the money the company deposited will be yours. You typically need to work with a company for three to five years before you become fully vested.

Although you cannot use the money that is in your 401(k) plan until you leave the program or retire, many plans will allow you to borrow against it for serious life events. Examples of a serious life event would be to purchase a home or if you have a health-related problem.

Pension Plans

Pension plans are another type of retirement savings plans some companies offer. Usually pension plans consist of specific amounts of money the company will automatically save for you. You do not pay any money into these plans. Pension plans are less common than 401(k) plans.

Stock Options

Some companies offer stock options as an additional benefit for their employees. In this case, the company will purchase shares of company stock for their employees as a part of their compensation package. You may also have the option to buy stock in the company at a lower rate than the market offers.

Additional Benefits

Sick Days

Some employers provide sick days off for theiremployees to use when they or their children are sick.

Vacation Days

Typically after a specific period of service, you will be eligible for vacation time. Most companies allow you to earn vacation time. You will need to notify your employer in advance if you plan to use vacation time. Each company has specific guidelines about the use of vacation time. Some companies even have "blackout dates," or specific days when you cannot use your vacation time. Blackout dates usually fall during the busiest time of year for your company.

Holidays

Many companies give time off on national and major holidays. Certain industries may require you to work on those days. Days like Thanksgiving, Christmas, Memorial Day, Labor Day, and the Fourth of July are common holidays. Some companies will pay you extra for working on a holiday!

Paid Time Off

Paid time off, also known as **PTO** days, are additional vacation days an employee can earn during their employment. These days can be used for whatever reason an employee wants. They often take the place of sick days, holidays, and vacation days. For example, for every month you work, you could earn one PTO day.

Funeral (Bereavement) Leave

Many companies will pay you for one to three days to attend a funeral. Some companies will only pay funeral leave if an immediate family member passes away. Immediate family members usually include:

- Parents
- Grandparents
- Spouse
- Brothers or sisters
- Children.

Leaves of Absence

A leave of absence is an extended period of time you do not work. Most companies will provide you with various types of leaves of absence. Some leaves of absence are paid, and others are not. There are a few types the law requires employers to offer. Others are a benefit you may receive after you have worked for the company after a period of time.

Long-Term Leave of Absence

What if you have an event in your life that requires you to be gone from the job for a long time? Some companies will allow you to take long periods of time off. They do not pay you during this time, but they may agree to hold your job for you. Be sure to talk about your need with your manager.

Family Medical Leave Act

Under certain situations, employees may qualify for **Family Medical Leave (FML)**. FML is available for the birth of a child, an employee's serious health condition, or a serious health condition affecting a spouse, child, or parent you would need to care for. There is a maximum of 12 weeks allowed during a 12-month period. This is unpaid leave.

Summary

Benefits are designed to be added incentives for you to work for a company. Be sure to fully understand your benefits. When deciding between jobs, comparing the benefit package that is offered is important. The long-term payoff of benefits can be significant.

There are times when an employee may have to choose whether or not to take advantage of a benefit. Be sure to fully investigate the benefits that are offered to you. In many cases, the cost of the benefit will be much lower than the cost of not having the benefit. Remember that serious illnesses can be very expensive.

Glossary

Beneficiaries: the people you choose to receive money from an insurance policy.

Benefits: extra services or features besides money which an employer offers to employees.

Co-pay: the portion of the cost of a doctor's visit that you have to pay.

Deductible: a predetermined amount of money you pay before your insurance coverage will begin payment.

Direct deposit: when your company deposits your paycheck into your personal checking or savings account.

Family Medical Leave (FML): unpaid leave time for workers, available for the birth of a child, an employee's serious health condition, or a serious health condition affecting a spouse, child, or parent you would need to care for.

Federal income tax: you pay a percentage of your income based upon tax law.

FICA: 7.5% of your paycheck goes to the Social Security office. Your employer matches that amount. This money comes out of your paycheck each time you are paid. You can request a summary of your social security account from the Social Security office.

401(k): a pretax retirement plan where you can contribute to a retirement fund by having the money taken out of your paycheck. The name refers to the section of U.S. Tax Code authorizing the plan.

Generic drugs: drugs sold under their chemical name that contain the same active ingredients as brand-name drugs, but are less expensive.

HMO (Health Maintenance Organization): an HMO is a group of doctors that join together to form an organization.

Internal Revenue Service (IRS): the government agency in charge of the collection of taxes.

Leave of absence: an extended period of time that you do not work.

Life insurance: an optional benefit you may choose to carry that will be paid to your beneficiaries when you die.

Local income tax: may also be required depending on the local tax laws.

Pension plan: a retirement plan consisting of specific amounts of money a company will automatically save for you.

Perk: something extra you get other than your base salary.

POS (Point of Service): a POS allows you to choose any doctor you want, but generally pays less of the costs than does an HMO or a PPO.

PPO (Preferred Provider Organization): a PPO allows you to choose a doctor from an approved listing of doctors provided by your insurance company.

Prescription drug card: a card issued by an insurance company which you show at a pharmacy to get a lower cost for prescription drugs.

Pretax option: your benefits are automatically taken out of your paycheck before taxes are calculated on your income.

PTO days: paid time off, extra vacation days awarded for achievements like perfect attendance or for length of service.

Referral: when a doctor recommends you visit another doctor, typically a specialist.

Self-Employment tax: If you are self-employed, you pay a self-employment tax of 15%.

State income tax: many states also require you to pay taxes on the money you earn.

Stock options: a benefit where employees are either paid with company stock rather than money or are offered the opportunity to purchase company stock at a reduced price.

Taxes: extra fees charged on goods and property you buy and the money you earn.

Term life insurance: money will only be paid to your beneficiaries if you die while you are paying the policy premiums.

Vesting schedule: a plan which requires you to work for a company for a certain number of years before you can fully use any money the company has contributed to your 401(k) or pension plan.

W-2 statement: lists how much you earned in the previous year and how much tax you paid.

Exercises

1. Internet Exercise (see Pages 209-210 for more information on the Internet): Log on to any search engine (www.google.com, www.dogpile.com, www.yahoo.com) and search by the following terms to learn more about benefits.

    - Benefits insurance
    - Savings plans
    - Pensions
    - 401(k) plans
    - Pretax benefits
    - Life and health insurance
    - PPO
    - HMO
    - Cafeteria insurance plans
    - Federally mandated job benefits
    - Family Medical Leave Act.

2. Research two jobs with two different companies you may be interested in applying for. Which one offers more? It may not be the job that has a higher salary. Take the time to research the company's benefits packages. The Internet is a useful tool for this.

CHAPTER 15

COMMUNICATION AT WORK

Everybody communicates in one way or another. Communicating well at work is the key to success. The greetings, information, questions, ideas, and comments you make all reflect upon you. Even how you handle conflict can determine your success. Communication takes many forms – listening, speaking, and writing.

Learn to Listen

Listening is considered by many to be the most important part of communication. Learning how to listen is a critical part of your success. Start by truly paying attention to what the speaker is saying—this includes making eye contact. This can include watching the person speaking, keeping an open mind (don't judge until you hear it all,) and putting together more than one idea. Listening can be hard work. Do not be afraid to take notes if you need to keep track of what was said.

Ways to Check if You Understood

Use phrases and questions to clarify and verify the message:

- "Would you mind repeating what you said again? I'm not sure I got it all."
- "Let me see if I can restate what you said..."
- "Could you say what you said another way please?"

Some speakers will repeat exactly what he or she said, only louder. Just because a person says the message was not clear—it does not

> **IN THIS CHAPTER**
> - Learning to listen
> - Speaking clearly
> - Using questions
> - Learning to write
> - Proper communication with your boss
> - Communicating with co-workers
> - Conflict resolutions in the workplace

mean he or she cannot hear. Do not be afraid to seek more information to answer the questions you have by listening.

Immigrant Views

"I ask my friends to be sure to tell me when my words are wrong. Sometimes my language is backwards - I might say things like 'let's eat at the court food.' No, it's suppose to be food court."

Khulood Ankrom is a naturalized citizen working in the hotel industry.

Speaking Clearly

The speaker sends the message. Stay focused on what you want to get across. In addition to learning the language, there is the speaking of the language.

Tips for speaking clearly:

- Be clear in your own mind what you want to say.
- Keep your message simple.
- Check to see if the listener understood. You may need to ask a question or wait for a reply to your message.
- Say what you mean. You can still be polite.
- Repeat the action points of your message to clarify expectations or requests.

Use Questions to Manage Workplace Communication

How do you know the right question to ask? Easy—what do you want to know? There are several types of questions to use to get different responses. Below is a chart of question types and examples of each.

Question	Example
Feedback—to find out how you are doing	Question: Do you think the training helped this department?
Follow-Up—to get more information or an opinion	Question: Is this a positive report compared to the last time?

Question	Example
Open—does not invite a particular answer, but opens things up for discussion	Question: How do think the team will view this event?
Closed—is very specific to get a "yes or no" response	Question: Do you ever read the weather page in the newspaper?
Fact-Finding—is aimed at getting information on a particular subject	Question: What percentage of your department went through yesterday's training?

Learning What to Write

There are several keys to success when using written communication. Writing in the workplace can take several forms—e-mail, memos, reports or letters. No matter what the written communication, there are several things to know for good writing:

+ Keep your message clear
+ Check your spelling and grammar
+ Follow prescribed formats from your company or standard practice
+ Proof your work
+ Summarize your key points
+ Give appropriate details such as "who, what, where, when, and how."

Talking to the Boss

Do not be afraid to ask questions of your boss or manager.

When you greet someone at home, you may do so with a hug. In the workplace, a hug is not appropriate. It is better to use a firm handshake and a smile.

When you want to communicate with your boss, it is appropriate to ask him or her when you could have an opportunity to talk. In some offices, it is appropriate to make a formal appointment. When it is time to speak with your boss, make sure you are there on time and prepared for the discussion. Typically, when meeting with your boss, you should use more formal language. Do not use slang.

Immigrant Views

"I'm not American, so certain things I approach differently. Sometimes I try to sit down and talk with my boss and explain certain things. I always ask him about his feedback - 'what do you think about...? Am I saying it clear enough for you to understand?'"

Khulood Ankrom is a naturalized citizen working in the hotel industry.

Talking to Your Co-Workers

Sometimes it can be difficult to adjust to a new work environment. When you are from a different culture and feel unsure, it can be even more difficult. There are several things you can do that can help build relationships with your co-workers. These include:

- Always be friendly
- Greet co-workers whenever you see them
- Sit with co-workers at lunch or on breaks
- Start a conversation.

People are usually more willing to build friendships with people who seem to be happy and positive. To Americans, you can seem friendly by greeting them when you see them, even if it is just with a smile.

You might be surprised to learn other people feel as shy around you as you might feel around them. Try to take the first step. Sit with a co-worker or invite a co-worker to sit with you. A good way to get to know someone is to try to start a conversation. If others tell you about themselves, they will expect you to share a little about yourself as well. The hard part is getting started!

Be friendly with co-workers.

Resolving Conflict

Whenever there is more than one person in a room, there is a chance for disagreement. In America, it is acceptable to disagree with someone. What is important is how you present your opinion. Dealing with **conflict** when someone disagrees with you is an extremely important skill.

What do you do when you have a problem at work?

- Be willing to listen to others' opinions
- Pick an appropriate time to talk about the problem
- Stay calm and level-headed
- Explain how you understand the situation
- Focus on the issue or problem
- Be flexible.

Willingness to talk about disagreements is the key to solving problems. If problems are not discussed, a person can become so frustrated they might even quit their job!

It is also important to pick the appropriate time to discuss problems. It is not acceptable to discuss issues in front of a customer. If you have something to discuss, it should always be done in private.

Try to control your emotions when resolving conflicts. You will get the best results if you stay calm. As you explain how you feel to the other person, focus on the problem, not the person. Describe your feelings. For example:

The right way: I feel I am not respected for the work I do because ...

The wrong way: You do not respect me.

Notice the right way focuses on you and your feelings. In the wrong way, it seems as though you are accusing the other person. It is important to keep the discussion focused on the issue at hand. Do not allow the discussion to become personal.

After you have shared your feelings, be ready to listen to the other person's opinion. Listening carefully and understanding the other person's point of view is extremely important. If people feel as though their side has not been heard, they get defensive and less willing to work it out together. Compromise is a key concept in resolving problems.

Once both sides have been heard, try to solve the problem together. Try to solve the problem in a way both people will be happy or satisfied. Keep in mind you do not always have to agree with one another, but you do have to be willing to work together.

Talking to the Customer

In America, good customer service is always expected. There are some basic rules to follow regardless of where you work or what your job is. If you encounter a customer, remember:

- Greet every customer with a smile
- Greet or welcome customers whenever possible
- Take care of the customer's needs
- Try to go above and beyond what the customer expects
- Always thank customers for their business
- Always say goodbye.

Electronic Communication

In many areas of the country, and in many companies, **electronic communication** (through e-mail, instant messaging, or chat rooms) is becoming very common.

E-Mail

When sending or replying to e-mail at work, you should always follow some basic rules:

- Do not use slang
- Do not type in all capitals: TYPING IN ALL CAPITAL LETTERS IS CONSIDERED TO BE YELLING!
- Keep your e-mail short and to the point
- Never share personal information
- Avoid sending personal mail like jokes or gossip.

Language on E-Mail

While the language used in e-mail can be less formal than that in a traditional written letter, be sure to avoid words or phrases that might be offensive. E-mail is not considered to be private and can be sent to other people very easily. Sometimes e-mails can even be sent accidentally. Never type anything you would not want someone else to read. E-mail does not have the same impact as a personal conversation.

Summary

Communicating well is a key to success and includes listening, speaking, and writing. Learning to listen is a skill. Following a well-organized process, you can speak effectively. Questions are important when communicating in the workplace. The principles for writing in the workplace include keeping your message clear, checking your spelling and grammar, as well as summarizing key points.

Regardless of who you are talking to or what method of communication you are using in the workplace, it is important to remember to:

- Be professional
- Be polite
- Be positive
- Be open to new ideas.

Do not be afraid to take the first step in the communication process. If you want to meet someone, or even if you have a conflict with someone, it is appropriate to approach them as long as you do so with respect.

Glossary

Closed-ended question: is very specific to get a yes or no answer.

Communication: exchange of thoughts, messages, or information, by speech, signals, writing, or behavior.

Conflict: a disagreement or opposition.

Electronic communication: exchange of thoughts, messages, or information through the computer either by e-mail, instant messaging, or chat rooms.

Fact-finding question: is used to get additional information on a particular subject.

Feedback question: used to find out how you are performing.

Follow-up question: used to get additional information.

Open-ended question: does not invite a particular answer, but allows for discussion.

Exercises

1. Internet Exercise (see Pages 209-210 for more information on the Internet): Log on to any search engine (www.google.com, www.dogpile.com, www.yahoo.com) and search by the following terms to learn more about communication in the workplace.

    - Proper communication at work
    - Conflict resolution
    - Taking care of the customer
    - Electronic communication.

2. Get two friends and role play (act out) the following conflicts:

    a. One person is the customer, another is the employee and the third is an observer. The customer does not like the product he/she has been given and wants to return it without the receipt. Store policy says only store credit can be given without a receipt. The customer only wants cash. Resolve the conflict!

    b. One person is the employee, another is the boss, and the third is an observer. The employee does not like the schedule he/she has been given and wants to get it changed. The boss does not want to change the schedule. Resolve the conflict!

    c. One person is employee A, another person is employee B, and the third person is a manager. Employee A feels employee B is always given the easier job. Employee B disagrees. The manager has to resolve the conflict!

Chapter 16

Telephones and Other Technology

Twenty years ago, computers were a luxury item. Now, more than 50% of all Americans have a computer in their home.

In America, some people have technology, others do not. People who have access to computers, cable TV, and the Internet have the opportunity to get better jobs, better education, and better success. Our government is working to give all people access to technology.

This chapter will look at some of the basic equipment and services found in the American home.

Telephone

Telephones

In the last 15 years, the United States went from having one big phone company to having several smaller regional companies. There is now competition for long-distance phone services.

Your Local Phone Company

In America, almost everyone has at least one telephone. Each house has its own phone line that is not shared with anyone else. Your local phone company provides basic phone services and local phone service. Another company provides long-distance service.

> **In This Chapter**
>
> - Basic and local phone service
> - Choosing a long-distance provider
> - International phone service
> - How phone cards work
> - Cellular phones
> - Pagers
> - Phone technology in the workplace

Americans use phones to connect with people at work, for business, and to talk with friends and family.

Your local phone bill includes one basic monthly charge for:

+ Receiving calls
+ Being listed in the telephone directory
+ Making **local calls** (calls within your city or city area).

Your monthly bill also includes taxes and charges for local services.

Phone Basics

Phone numbers in the United States contain 10 digits.

A three-digit area code indicating your location in the United States, and a personal seven-digit number. Example: **(317) 555-5555**

Local calls—Some areas of the country require "10-digit dialing." This means you need to dial all 10 digits of a phone number (including the area code) to make a local call. Other areas allow you to dial only the last seven digits of a phone number to make a local call. Example: **555-5555** or **(317)555-5555**

Long Distance—If you want to call someone outside your area code, you need to dial 1 + (area code) + number. Example: **1-(317)-555-5555**

Toll Free—These calls are free. Numbers with an area code of 800, 888, 877, and 866 are paid by the owner of the number. Example:**1-800-444-4444**

Collect Call—To make a **collect call** (a call that is charged to the person you are calling), you need to dial 0 for the operator. Tell the operator you want to make a collect call. They will ask for the phone number you want to call. They will call the number and ask the person who answers if they will accept the charges. The charges for your call will be charged to his or her phone bill.

Setting Up Service—Contact the local phone company to establish new service. They will assign a phone number. You may have to put down a **deposit** (pay a larger amount on your first bill). You will be billed once every month. You can lease a phone from the telephone company for a monthly fee. You can also buy a phone at a store.

If You Move—If you move within the same city or town, you may be able to keep your phone number. You will need to change your billing information. If you get a new phone number, be sure to tell your employer, along with your friends and family. You should also tell anyone else who may need to contact you, such as other companies you pay monthly bills to or your doctor.

Long-Distance Phone Service

Long-distance phone service usually comes from a different company than your local phone service. Your long-distance company will handle any calls you make that are outside your area. You call these areas by dialing 1 + the 10-digit phone number. Each phone call you make is charged based on:

- The time of day (day, evening, or night)
- The day of the week (weekday or weekend)
- The place you are calling (intrastate, interstate, or international)
- The cost of your long-distance plan.

Calls made within your state are called **intrastate** calls. Calls made to another state are called **interstate** calls. There are different tariffs and taxes on these calls, and companies usually have different rates for each. **International** calls are calls made to a different country. The rates of international calls will vary based on the country.

Some companies will charge a higher rate for calls made during the day and will offer lower rates in the evening or at night. Weekend rates are often cheaper than weekday rates.

There is a great deal of competition among long-distance companies. Many offer a flat rate, 24 hours a day, seven days a week for the same price per minute. Pay attention to additional service charges, or minimum call charges. You may be charged a set fee each month, even if you do not make any calls.

Billing

When you use certain long-distance companies, you can receive one bill for both your local and long-distance charges. Other long-distance companies will charge you on separate bills.

International Calling

Most international phone calls from North America require you to dial the access code 011 + country code + city code + local number + telephone number. The following website has a list of international country and city codes. http://www.countrycallingcodes.com/

International calls can be expensive. Take the time to research different companies to see who offers the best rate to the country you will call most often. Ask friends and family members living in the United States what rates they pay and what companies they use.

Phone Cards

Phone cards are used when you are traveling or are not calling from your home. Each card has a toll free phone number you will need to call and a **PIN number** (access number) you will need to enter in order to make a call. Follow the instructions on the card to enter the phone number you want to reach. Your number will then be dialed.

There are two types of phone cards:

- **Prepaid cards** – You buy a card with a certain amount of minutes available and use the card until it is out of call time. Anyone can use a prepaid card, so you can give them as gifts or to family members. Prepaid cards can be purchased for a low rate. You may be able to save money on international calls with prepaid cards. Every card is different, so check the rates and calling destinations before you buy the card. You may have extra fees added to each call. **Rates: 5 to 12 cents per minute.**

- **Non-Prepaid cards** – You can get calling cards from your local phone company or your long-distance company. Any calls you make with these cards are billed to you on your next bill. This can be a good option if you do not want to purchase a prepaid card. The rates on calls made with the card can be much higher than your normal phone rates. **Rates: 39 to 90 cents per minute.**

Both types of phone cards are easy to get and use.

Dial 10-10-xxx

You may see ads on television that promote low phone rates when you dial 10-10 this and 10-10 that on calls under, over, or between 20 minutes. So what are these 10-10-xxx numbers and how do they work?

When you dial a 10-10-xxx number, you are using another long-distance company to make your phone call. You will be billed by this company for each call you make. It may appear on your local phone bill, or it may come as a separate bill.

You need to look at the 10-10-xxx plans just like you would a normal long-distance service. You may have additional monthly fees or minimum calling times. There are times when a 10-10-xxx plan may help you save money. For example, a specific 10-10-xxx plan may have great rates to Germany, while your normal long-distance company has very poor rates to Germany, but great rates within the United States. You may choose to use the 10-10-xxx service for those calls to Germany while using your primary carrier for calls in the United States.

900 numbers

Numbers with an area code of 900 are used in ads to provide information or entertainment. When you dial a 900 number, you are charged an initial fee for calling, along with a high, per-minute rate. The charge for the call will appear on your monthly local phone bill. Be very careful when calling 900 numbers and never call them from a work phone. The company you are calling makes money from the phone charges.

Directory Assistance

If you do not know the number or cannot find the number in the phone book, Directory Assistance can help you. For local and nationwide numbers dial 1 + 411 or 1+Area Code+555-1212. For 800, 888, 877, and 866 numbers, dial 1+800+555-1212.

You will need to give the operator the name of the city and person or company you wish to call. The operator will then be able to give you the phone number. For an additional fee, they can connect your call. A charge may apply on calls to Directory Assistance.

Telephone Solicitation

Telemarketing calls are calls you receive but did not request. Telemarketers are people who work for a company. **Telemarketers** call people and try to sell them products or services. They usually read from a prepared script. If you are not interested in what they are selling or you do not understand what they want, you can interrupt them and tell them you are not interested.

When you get a telemarketing call:

- If you are not interested, interrupt them and tell them you are not interested.
- You can hang up at any time. You do not have to listen to the whole speech.
- If you do not understand everything they are saying, ask them to send written material to you.

Pay Phones

You will find pay phones in many public buildings, at gas stations, and along the street. Look for a blue sign with a phone. Pay phones use coins, calling cards, or credit cards for payment. You can also dial 0 (zero) and ask the operator to place the call for you. That will cost more than dialing the number directly. If you are making a local phone call within the current area code, you can usually talk for an unlimited amount of time for 35 to 50 cents. Long-distance calls cost more. If you are using coins, you may need to pay more money during or after your call. Using a calling card is the easiest option for making long-distance calls from a pay phone.

Pay Phone Sign

Cellular Phones

A **cellular phone** is a mobile phone you can carry with you. You can make calls from your home, work, or your car. Today, cellular phones are used by professionals, students, workers, parents, and children. Some Americans choose not to have a phone in their home and only use their cellular phone.

Americans will use their cell phones from anywhere. Be aware, however, many cities have laws making it illegal to use a cell phone while driving. Cellular phones purchased in America will only work in the United States and in some places in Mexico.

Here is a list of features that should be considered when looking for a cell phone:

- Service plan
- Coverage area
- Daily rates
- Night and weekend rates
- Mode
- Battery type
- Display
- Special features
- Size
- Price.

Cell phones are common in America.

There are many great websites available for learning about the latest cell phone accessories, providers, and plans. Ask your local providers and shop for the best plan.

Check out this website for a comparison of cell phones and services: http://www.getconnected.com/

Pagers

A **pager** is a small device that can be hooked over a belt or carried in a pocket and allows the wearer to receive a caller's phone number or a short message. The message you send may be a short sentence or a phone number. Paging is a good option when you want to send someone a quick message or have someone return a call to you. At one time, pagers were only used by doctors or emergency personnel. Pagers are now used by many Americans. Companies also use them to contact employees when they are away from a phone. Children and teens also use pagers so parents and friends can contact them.

Pagers help you keep in touch with others.

To page someone, you need to dial their pager number (a phone number that activates their pager). You will then need to enter the number you want them to call. Some pagers will allow you to leave a voice or text message as well. The pager will beep or buzz, and the person can look at the display to see the message number or message. Some pagers allow you to type a short message on the provider's website. The message is sent to the pager.

Fax Machines

A **fax machine** (short for facsimile) allows you to send copies of documents over the phone to another fax machine. Faxes are great for sending printed documents, forms, and applications. Fax machines have become an important business tool in most offices. You will even find restaurants use fax machines to receive take-out orders. You can fax in your lunch order so they will have it ready for you to pick up when you arrive! Faxes do not print in color, and the quality of the printout may be hard to read.

Fax Machine

Many small printers' shops, such as Kinko's©, and shipping services like Mailboxes Etc…© and The Box Shop©, have fax machines you can use for a fee. They have staff who can help you with the process. Most employers will allow you to send a fax from work, if needed. Check with your supervisor or manager.

Technology in the Workplace

When you are using technology at work, there are some basic rules you should follow. Do not use the phone at work for personal calls without permission, except in case of an emergency.

Answering the Telephone

When answering the telephone at work, it is important to be polite. Here are good tips for talking on the phone:

- Answer the phone with a positive greeting… "Good Morning," "Good Afternoon," etc.
- You may want to smile as you talk. People on the phone will hear how friendly you are and that you are willing to help.
- Identify the company and yourself. Then ask how you can help them. For example: "Good Morning. XYZ Company. This is Pedro. How may I help you?"
- You may not be able to help the person on the phone. Ask them if you can place them on hold and get someone who can.
- If you need to take a message, make sure you collect the information you need:
  - Caller's first name
  - Caller's phone number (including area code)
  - What time they called
  - Who they are calling
  - Why they are calling.
- Once you have written all the information down, read it back to the caller to ensure the information is correct.
- After making sure the information is correct, ask the caller if you can do anything else for them.
- Finally, thank the caller for calling and say "Goodbye."

Cell Phones and Pagers

It is not unusual for people to carry cell phones and beepers with them at all times. Check with your company to find out what the policy is for carrying these items. Some companies have strict rules about the use of personal cell phones and beepers.

Summary

Technology can help you communicate more efficiently. Communication technology changes all the time. Understanding the different options that are available to help you communicate will assist you to become independent. Technology can make your life easier. You may also find you have to learn about new forms of communication in order to succeed in your job. Take the time to research all your options and choose the ones that work best for you.

Communication in the workplace can be very different from communicating with family or friends. How you greet people, how and when you talk to your boss, and how you handle a disagreement are some things to consider.

Glossary

Cell phone: a mobile phone you can carry with you.

Collect call: a call that is charged to the person you are calling.

Deposit: an amount added to your first telephone bill to cover the cost of establishing the service.

Fax machine: short for facsimile machine, a device that allows you to send copies of documents over the phone to another fax machine.

International calls: calls made to a different country.

Interstate calls: calls made to another state.

Intrastate calls: calls made within your state.

Local calls: calls within your city or city area.

Long distance: a call made to someone outside your area code.

Non-Prepaid phone card: a card issued by a local or long-distance phone company that allows calls to be billed to the caller's home phone.

Pager: a small device that can be hooked over a belt or carried in a pocket and allows the wearer to receive a caller's phone number or a short message. Sometimes called a "beeper."

PIN: Personal Identification Number, a code set by the phone card issuer to allow use of the phone card.

Prepaid phone card: a card with a set amount of minutes available that is used until it is out of call time.

Telemarketers: people whose job is to call people and try to sell them products or services.

Toll Free: phone numbers with an area code of 800, 888, 877, and 866 are paid for by the owner of the number.

Exercises

1. Internet Exercise (see Pages 209-210 for more information on the Internet): Log on to any search engine (www.google.com, www.dogpile.com, www.yahoo.com) and search by the following terms to learn more about telephones and other technology. For many of these, you may choose to put the name of the city or state you live in before the word or phrase. Doing this will bring up local information as well as national information.

    + Local telephone services
    + How to use a phone
    + Long-distance phone service providers
    + International phone service providers
    + Phone cards
    + 1-800
    + 1-900
    + U.S. directory assistance
    + How to use a pay phone
    + Cellular phones
    + www.getconnected.com
    + Pagers

2. Comparison-shop the different long-distance carriers that are available to you. You will need to remember to seek out both the international and the domestic rates. Some will offer specific rates to your home country. And what about time zones? Which carrier is more affordable for the time you will be using the phone the most?

Chapter 17

Mass Communication

Listening, reading, or watching news reports about current events is a good way to continue to learn English. This will also help you become more familiar with American culture. Television (TV), radio, newspapers, magazines, and the Internet can keep you current on the things happening in your neighborhood and around the world. You can choose from hundreds of TV programs, newspapers, magazines, and websites. These are all filled with information, music, and entertainment. This chapter takes a look at some of your options when it comes to the media.

Television (TV)

America is known for its movies and television programs. Many people have their only impression of the United States from movies and television shows they have viewed. Most Americans are not like the characters you see in films and on television.

Watching TV is a good way to learn about the United States.

In This Chapter

- American television offers many options
- Cable television offers even more options
- American television programming
- Listening to the radio
- Print media: Newspapers and magazines
- The Internet is a tool for learning and entertainment

Television Access

In the United States, you can access TV channels in several ways:

Connection	Channels	Features
Antenna – The signal comes in through an antenna attached to the TV	Major networks, Public television, Local religious programming	Free. You usually only have 8-10 channels available.
Cable – The cable company runs a cable to your house or apartment	Many choices of programming	You pay a monthly fee based on the programs you choose. You can choose from basic cable with a small number of channels, to all the channels, plus premium channels, and pay-per-view programs.
Satellite TV – satellite dish at your home connects to a satellite	First used in rural areas where cable TV was not available. Now it is more affordable and many people have it.	You pay a monthly fee. You must buy or rent the satellite dish.

Network Programming

Network programming features a wide variety of shows including:

- News
- Entertainment
- Music
- Sports.

In the United States there are several national television networks that can be viewed across the country without having to pay for cable or satellite TV:

- ABC
- NBC
- CBS
- FOX

- **Local TV** stations are each affiliated with a national network. They provide local and national news, entertainment programs, sports, music, specials, soap operas, cartoons, game shows, drama, and comedy shows. Programming is supported by commercial advertising.
- **Commercials** promoting different products are shown throughout programs.
- **Shows are rated**; shows may be modified to remove sex, foul language, and violence.

Rating	Audience
Y	All Children
Y7	Children 7 and above
G	Everyone - general audience
PG	Parental Guidance
14	Not suitable for children under 14
MA	Mature audience - not for children under 17

- **PBS** - Public Broadcasting Service
  - A non-profit organization providing educational programming, documentaries, children's programming, arts, drama, comedy, and music
  - There are no commercials on Public TV, programming is supported by contributions and sponsorship by business and the public
  - Have pledge drives twice a year to earn support
  - Generally all-around family entertainment.

Cable TV

Many American households have cable TV. **Cable TV** signal comes through a cable rather than airwaves. Cable TV provides you with more channels to choose from and provides a higher quality picture. You pay a monthly fee to subscribe to cable.

You may get a **converter box** that goes between the cable and your TV. This box allows you to receive additional "premium" cable channels. **Premium channels** feature recently released movies and specials. Premium channels are available at an additional charge. **Pay-per-view** channels are also available. These allow you to watch a movie or special for a set fee. You can also restrict access to certain channels if you want to control what channels your children may watch.

Cable programming provides a wide variety of channels. Many of the channels are geared toward specific groups or interests. Some of the channels include programs on:

- Sports
- News
- History
- Animals
- Science
- Home and garden
- Travel
- Science fiction
- Comedy
- Different ethnic groups
- Music
- Theatre
- Movies

Types of Television Programs

There are many different types of programs available on TV.

News Programs

Read the TV!

Many newer TV sets now include a feature called **closed-captioning**, that displays the text of what is being said on the screen. As people speak you can read the words and begin to learn the language.

Most news coverage is focused on the United States and its involvement with the rest of the world.

The major networks generally have a combination of local news and national news programs throughout the day. In addition, most networks have one or two news magazine programs that are shown once or twice a week. Cable TV offers many news-only channels that feature around-the-clock news coverage. Some of these channels include CNN, CNN Headline News, FNN, CNBC, MSNBC, and Fox News Network.

Talk Shows

Many Americans are interested in other people and their lives. Those people tend to enjoy daytime talk shows. These programs often pick a topic to discuss and have guests on the show who have experience with that topic.

Some of the most popular daytime and late night shows feature celebrity guests, along with music and humor. Other talk shows on TV are designed to get people to watch by choosing dramatic or sensational topics. Some of the behaviors on sensational talk shows can be outrageous. These programs do not always show typical American people.

Game Shows

Game shows feature contests where people compete for prizes. Watching game shows can help you learn English. Game shows often feature items and supplies you use every day. You can also learn more about the value of the American dollar by watching game shows.

Radio

The radio is another great way to listen to the English language and learn about America. There are many stations from which to choose. Popular radio formats include different types of music stations. Some types of music stations include:

- Rock music
- Easy listening
- Country
- Classical
- Urban
- Rap
- Alternative
- Jazz.

Some radio stations do not play music at all. They may feature news and discussion programs. These stations are called **Talk Radio** stations. Still other radio stations offer a combination of both talk and music.

Listen to the radio to improve your English.

Many people in America listen to the radio while driving or commuting to and from work. This can be a great time to listen to people talking about many different topics. Listening to talk radio is a great way to expand your vocabulary.

American radio stations are available in AM and FM formats. AM and FM differ in the way the stations broadcast radio signals. AM stations have greater range, but the quality of the broadcast is not as strong as an FM broadcast. Many talk radio stations are AM stations. FM stations have a stronger, more direct signal. FM broadcasts have a limited range and feature more music programs.

Most of the stations are commercial supported. That means they have advertisements and commercials. NPR (National Public Radio) stations are commercial-free and feature news, music, and discussion programs.

Newspapers and Magazines

Looking for a Job? Check out the Sunday Paper!

Most employers run job openings in the Sunday newspaper. The ads are organized by type of job, usually professional, technical, clerical, sales, medical, and trade. Most ads indicate the position, some responsibilities or requirements needed for the job and how to contact the employer.

Newspapers are a good source of information. Every major city in the United States has a daily newspaper. Many smaller towns may also have a daily or weekly paper.

There are several nationally distributed newspapers. Some nationally distributed newspapers include the *USA Today* and the *Wall Street Journal.* These newspapers are distributed for sale on weekdays (Monday – Friday) across the country.

Some of the larger cities also distribute their city paper nationally. Examples include *The Washington Post*, *New York Times*, and the *Chicago Tribune*. Local papers usually focus on local events, with some national and international news. Even though a newspaper may be distributed nationally, the version of the paper distributed in each region may differ slightly. Newspaper companies try to customize the newspapers to the interest and events of the region.

The Sunday edition of the paper is usually twice as large as the weekday paper. Sunday papers often include special stories and features, including:

+ Employment ads
+ Grocery coupons
+ Advertisements from local stores
+ Color cartoons

Newspapers provide world, national, and local news and stories.

- Expanded real estate, travel, and automotive sections.

It is a good idea to buy a Sunday paper when you are looking for a job or a place to live.

Magazines are another resource for learning about America and the English language. You can go to any bookstore, supermarket, or newsstand and you will find hundreds of magazines. Magazines cover almost every topic and hobby. General news magazines review what is going on in America and in the world. Choose a magazine that interests you and read it on a regular basis.

You can find magazines about almost anything.

The Internet

The Internet is quickly becoming one of the best sources for news, information, and entertainment. If you have a computer, a modem, and an Internet connection, you can have access to many of the major newspapers online. You can also listen to radio programs on the Internet and find information about almost anything.

> Don't have a computer? Check your local public library. Many libraries provide free access to the Internet!

Even if you do not own a computer, there are places you can get access to the Internet. Check out your local public library for free-use computers. The government is trying to make sure all people, regardless of their income level, have the ability to access information found on the Internet.

One of the great things about the Internet is the instant availability of news and information. You can find out what is going on faster than watching TV. Many of the news sites are also translated into other languages.

Internet Browsers and Search Engines

An Internet browser is a screen program that lets you view web pages and move around the Internet. More simply, a browser allows you to use the Internet from your computer. Common browsers include Netscape and Microsoft Explorer.

A search engine is a type of website. A search engine will look for websites on whatever topic you tell them to. If you want to learn about a certain subject try this:

1. Go to the search engine's home page (the page you will open up to).
2. Type in a word (keyword) or short phrase you want to know more about.
3. Click on the search key.
4. The search engine will list several websites that address the topic you are looking for.
5. Click on the website that best fits your need.

Search engines are very useful for researching almost any topic. There are many good sites for learning English as well. Do a search on the keyword "ESL", or phrase "English as a second language" on any search engine. You can also search for local ESL classes by adding the city you live in after the keyword, such as "ESL classes, Indianapolis."

Common Search Engines
- www.google.com
- www.dogpile.com
- www.yahoo.com
- www.search.com

Summary

The United States has many different ways of spreading information. Whether you listen to the radio, watch TV, surf the Internet, or read magazines and newspapers, you can find good information. Use the media to help you make a faster transition to the U.S. culture.

Glossary

Cable TV: signal comes through a cable rather than airwaves.

Converter box: a device that goes between the cable and your TV that provides additional services and channels.

Pay-per-view: allows you to watch a movie or special for a set fee.

Premium channels: feature recently released movies and specials. Premium channels are available at an additional charge.

Talk Radio: radio stations that feature news and discussion programs.

Exercises

1. Internet Exercise (see Pages 209-210 for more information on the Internet): Log on to any search engine (www.google.com, www.dogpile.com, www.yahoo.com) and search by the following terms to learn more about the media. For many of these, you may choose to put the name of the city or state you live in before the word or phrase. Doing this will bring up local information as well as national information.

   - American media
   - Television programming
   - Television guides
   - Cable television
   - Home entertainment
   - Radio stations
   - Newspapers
   - Magazines
   - How to use the Internet.

2. Watch the local news, listen to the radio, and read the paper for the same news story. Compare how different types of media handle the same story. The television news has the spoken word and video to impact you. The newspaper has the written word and photos to impact you. The radio has the spoken word and sounds to impact you. Which do you enjoy the most?

Chapter 18

Finding and Being a Mentor

It is easier to learn new things when you have a friend to help you. The same is true of transitioning to our culture and the American workplace. **Finding a mentor or a friend to help you through the changes is one of the best things you can do for yourself.**

Mentors Are There to Help You

A good mentor is someone who:

+ Can help explain things that are new or confusing
+ Can be honest with you about your progress
+ Can help you learn from your mistakes
+ Will be with you when you try new things.

As an immigrant, you need to accept suggestions and ideas without becoming angry or upset. A good friend and mentor will want you to succeed.

A **mentor** can help you with many of the things you will need to do when you first arrive in America. Some of the things a mentor can help you do more easily include:

+ Get through the immigration system
+ Learn about cleanliness and dress
+ Help you learn the language
+ Help you find a place to live
+ Explain customs, foods, transportation, shopping, and money.

In This Chapter

- What a mentor can do to help
- Setting up your relation with a mentor
- Networking and making friends

It can be helpful to find more than one mentor. You should also strive to make your mentor your friend. This will allow your mentors to relax and enjoy helping you.

Rules for the Mentor/Immigrant Relationship

Mentor and Immigrant

- Tell the truth
- Be patient
- Be open and communicate
- Listen carefully to each other and do not be offended by honest feedback
- Be direct.

For the Mentor

You do not have to be good at everything. If you do not have experience in a certain area, find someone who does.

Mentors can help you adjust to your new life.

Be sensitive to the appropriate time to provide correction. Avoid correcting the immigrant in front of others.

Include the immigrant in as many aspects of your daily life as you can. Try to do this for three to six months.

A Word from Kooner...

I've lived in the United States for about 20 years and have had many family members come over from India. I usually act as the mentor for the first year or so. My family member lives with me during the first year. We set up rules and I teach them the basics.

My nephew came from India last year. He lived with me for one year before living on his own. In living together, he learned the basics of keeping clean, how to dress, working with money, shopping for food, eating out, how to drive, making bigger purchases, how to manage his money, and dealing with different people.

Having a Family Member as a Mentor

Immediate family members (mothers, fathers, brothers, or sisters) who live in the United States are often your first choice for mentors. This can be good because they know and care about you. They also want you to succeed. Choosing a family member as a mentor can have its downfalls as well. Family members tend to be more direct and may not be as considerate of your feelings as a non-family member may be.

Sometimes an uncle, aunt, or cousin may be a better choice as a mentor. It may be easier for both of you to talk openly about things that might be more difficult to talk about with an immediate family member.

Small Groups and Organizations

Religious and social organizations are some of the best places to find a mentor. Attending religious services or social groups can put you in contact with people who will have something in common with you. You may be invited to dinners or social events where you can meet other people with similar interests or backgrounds. You should try to meet the executive board or committee members of religious or social organizations. These people may be able to connect you with people who can help you.

When you mentor new people, you are probably going to be asked questions about yourself and your background. Americans are curious about different people and cultures, and they tend to ask many questions. Be open and honest about yourself. Here are some common questions you may be asked:

- Where are you from? (your country)
- Why did you come here? (to America or to this city)
- Where are you living now? (neighborhood or area of city)
- What is your background? (occupation or experiences)
- What are your interests? (What do you like to do?)
- What is your family like? (Are you married, do you have children…?)

People ask questions to be polite and to get to know you. You can decide what you want to tell people about yourself. You may not feel comfortable answering all their questions. Feel free to politely tell them you would prefer not to talk about that subject.

Mentoring Activities

One of the best things a mentor can do is to let the new person follow you throughout your daily routine. Run **errands**, go shopping, and talk with people so they may better understand what typical American life is like. The immigrant can learn a lot by watching you and being allowed to ask questions. You can help the immigrant become familiar with the customs and culture in America. Teach the immigrant how to handle:

- Money
    - Talk about U.S. currency, its value, and how it compares to the money in his or her country
    - Teach him/her how to use cash
    - Set up a checking or savings account
    - Use a checkbook and balance a checkbook
    - Go shopping
    - Price items in weekly advertisements
    - Set up a budget
    - Set an allowance to help them learn how to buy things in America
    - Plan a trip
    - Plan for expenses.
- Communication
    - Say hello and goodbye
    - Introduce him or herself
    - Answer a phone
    - Leave a message on an answering machine
    - Use and understand American slang
    - Tell time.
- Socializing
    - Go to a dinner party
    - Go to a cocktail party
    - Go to a bar
    - Meet people of the opposite sex.
- Daily life
    - Act in an emergency
    - Make minor home repairs
    - Go to the doctor
    - Go to the dentist

- Go to the post office
- Clean the house
- Use appliances.

✦ Transportation
- Take a taxi ride
- Take a bus ride
- Take a train ride.

✦ Shopping
- Go grocery shopping
- Clothes shop
- Furniture shop
- Do household shopping
- Go to the mall
- Go to the drugstore
- Pick up a prescription
- Buy a car
- Buy and receive presents
- Discuss prices.

✦ Food
- Go to different restaurants
- Try different things
- Use place settings and different types of restaurants
- Order at a restaurant.

✦ Travel
- Make hotel reservations
- Rent a car
- Check into a hotel.

✦ Fun
- Go to movies
- Go to a sporting event
- Watch TV.

Summary

A mentor needs to be someone:

- You can learn from
- Who can teach you
- Who will be there when you need him or her.

A mentor is an important tool as you learn about the United States of America. Do not be afraid to ask questions. If you learn American English and U.S. history, you will have success.

Welcome to the American Workforce—We are glad you are here!

Glossary

Errands: a short trip to perform a specific task or tasks.

Immediate family members: your mother, father, brothers, and sisters.

Mentor: can help you with many of the things you will need to do when you first arrive in America.

Exercise

1. Internet Exercise (see Pages 209-210 for more information on the Internet): Log on to any search engine (www.google.com, www.dogpile.com, www.yahoo.com) and search by the following terms to learn more about mentoring. For many of these, you may choose to put the name of the city or state you live in before the word or phrase. Doing this will bring up local information as well as national information.

    - Mentoring
    - Helping a friend
    - Networking
    - Social organizations
    - Communicating
    - Socializing
    - Transportation
    - Travel.

2. Develop a mentor contract. After finding a mentor you need to come to an agreement on the roles each of you will play. Make a list of expectations you have for one another. Sit down with your mentor and discuss all of these points. Clarify, correct, and agree to the points on the list. If you do not have a formal mentor, you can go through the same process with a situational mentor.

Glossary

Accredited: a school approved or certified by an official organization.

Alien: people who are not citizens of the United States including permanent residents (green card holders), non-immigrants, asylees, refugees, parolees, and undocumented immigrants (illegal aliens).

Antiperspirant: cream or spray applied under the armpit to control sweat.

Assisted living facility: a hotel-type setting attached to, or near a care facility, where an elderly person can live independently with some daily or weekly assistance as needed.

Associate degree: a two-year degree offered by many colleges and universities that provides you with the training necessary to begin work.

Asylees: aliens who apply to INS for asylum, either after they enter or during entry to the United States, to avoid being persecuted in their home country.

ATM card: a card issued by a bank that, when used with a Personal Identification Number (PIN) of your choosing, allows you to use an automatic teller machine.

Auto loans: allow you to pay for a car in monthly installments.

Automatic Teller Machine (ATM): a device, usually located on a bank's property, that permits you to perform simple banking transactions without the aid of a human teller.

Baby-changing stations: changing tables usually hang on a wall and fold down from the wall. The table can be used to change a baby or young child's diaper.

Bachelor's degree: a four-year degree from a college or university.

Bar code: a marking printed on the label of a product to identify it and allow faster calculation of prices by the store register. Also known as a Universal Product Code (UPC).

Beneficiaries: the people you choose to receive the money from an insurance policy on you.

Benefits: extra services or features besides money which an employer offers to employees.

Budget: a monthly spending plan based on your income and expenses.

Buffet: a restaurant where, for a set price, you may take as much food as you want to eat. In general, you may take food only for yourself and unfinished food may not be taken home.

Business casual: more casual dress for work than a suit and tie. No suit, no tie, long pressed pants, not jeans, collared shirt for a man. A woman may vary her appearance with a skirt, casual shirt or blouse, typically wearing low-heeled shoes.

Cable TV: signal comes through a cable rather than airwaves.

Cafeteria: a restaurant where each item is individually plated and priced. You select the items you want.

Campground: an area reserved for tents or recreational vehicles to stay for a short period of time.

Cash: another name for currency.

Cashing a check: going to the bank and depositing your check or exchanging your paycheck for currency.

Catalog: a magazine or book containing pictures of, and information on, items being sold by a merchant along with directions on how to place an order with the merchant.

Cell phone: a mobile phone you can carry with you.

Certificate of deposit (CD): an account where you deposit your money with the bank for a certain length of time and they pay you a set interest rate.

Certification: extra training that will provide you with expertise in a specified area.

Chain restaurants: restaurants that go by the same name and serve similar food in cities all across the country.

Check: a paper, used in conjunction with a checking account, that identifies you and your account and authorizes a payee to receive the amount you specify from your account.

Checking account: a bank account from which funds may be drawn by the use of a check.

Citizen: any person who was born in the United States or who has been naturalized (granted full citizenship), unless they have given up their rights to citizenship in America.

Clinic: a medical office with a group of doctors.

Closing: is when you actually buy the house.

Closing costs: costs you pay in order to purchase a house, including down payments, escrow, commissions, and taxes.

Closed-ended question: is very specific to get a "yes" or "no" answer.

Collect call: a call that is charged to the person you are calling.

Communication: exchange of thoughts, messages, or information, by speech, signals, writing, or behavior.

Company culture: what a company believes in, its values, its focus, and the behaviors it expects and supports.

Conditioner: liquid used after shampoo to soften and untangle hair.

Condom: a form-fitting piece of latex designed to cover an erect penis. It is utilized to retain the sperm and keep body fluids from being exchanged. Condoms help minimize sexually transmitted diseases and pregnancy.

Conflict: a disagreement or opposition.

Consumers: the people who buy goods and services.

Continuing education classes: classes designed to teach very specific things to adults, such as English as a Second Language (ESL), typing skills, or how to use a specific software program.

Convenience store: a small store, often attached to a gas station, that concentrates on selling a selection of essential items for the convenience of their customers.

Conventional mortgage: requires you to put down 20% of the price of the house.

Converter box: a device that goes between the cable and your TV that provides additional services and channels.

Co-pay: a portion of the bill you need to pay when visiting the doctor or buying medicine.

County: local government.

Coupon: a small certificate, issued by a store or manufacturer, offering a product at a reduced price as an incentive to buy that product or shop in that store.

Cover letter: a letter expressing interest in a job and briefly explaining any qualifications.

Credit card: a plastic card issued by a bank which you can use instead of cash or a check to purchase items.

Credit rating: a record of how well you pay your bills.

Dandruff: flakes of dead skin in your hair.

Day care: a company licensed to watch children.

Debit card: a card issued by a bank and used like a credit card that functions as an electronic check.

Deductible: a predetermined amount of money you pay before your insurance coverage will begin payment.

Delivery: you place an order by phone and your food is delivered to your home.

Dental floss: coated string used to clean between teeth.

Deodorant: cream or spray applied under the armpit to control odor.

Department store: a store that sells a wide variety of non-food items.

Deposit: an amount added to your first telephone bill to cover the cost of establishing the service.

Destination sign: a sign on the front of a bus telling you where the bus is going.

Direct deposit: when your company deposits your paycheck into your personal checking or savings account.

Discount store: a store that concentrates on selling a selection of products at a lower price than elsewhere.

Discrimination: people judging others based on their appearance.

Dollar: the main unit of U.S. currency.

Down payment: the initial payment on a house.

Dress shoes: polished shoes, coordinated with the pants, skirt, or suit being worn by the person.

Drugstore/Pharmacy: a smaller store featuring a section for obtaining prescription drugs.

Dry cleaning: a chemical process for cleaning and pressing clothes that does not use water. Done by professionals in this service field.

Electronic communication: exchange of thoughts, messages, or information through the computer either by e-mail, instant messaging, or chat rooms.

Emergency medical team (EMT): people who staff an ambulance that answers calls for health emergencies.

Emergency room (ER): area of a hospital equipped to care for people with serious and immediate health needs.

Emissions test: a test, required in some states, to make sure your car does not produce too much pollution.

Employee pool: you are called when there is available work.

Equity: the money you pay toward your loan.

Errands: a short trip to perform a specific task or tasks.

Escrow account: an account where extra money is deposited from your mortgage payment, allowing you to pay small amounts toward taxes and insurance every month as part of your mortgage payment.

ESL: English as a Second Language.

Exact change: the precise amount of money needed to purchase your fare.

Exchange rate: the cost or benefit of exchanging the currency of your country for American money.

Exits: the ramps that allow you to leave an expressway.

Express lane: a lane for vehicles that do not need to exit the road for a long distance.

Expressways: roads that have many lanes for traffic.

Extended family: a family that has parents, grandparents, aunts, uncles, brothers, sisters, and children all living in the same, or in nearby, homes. Not common in the United States.

Fact-finding question: is used to get additional information on a particular subject.

Family Medical Leave (FML): unpaid leave time for workers, available for the birth of a child, an employee's serious health condition, or a serious health condition affecting a spouse, child, or parent you would need to care for.

Family style eating: where food is passed around the table.

Fare box: where you put your money or tokens to pay for a bus ride.

Farmer's market: a small group of farmers who sell fresh produce at a shared location.

Fast-food: a restaurant specializing in quick service of a limited selection of items at a low cost. Food may be eaten in the restaurant, carried out or you may go through a drive-through lane in your car to pick it up.

Fax machine: short for facsimile machine, a device that allows you to send copies of documents over the phone to another fax machine.

Federal income tax: you pay a percentage of your income based upon tax law.

Feedback question: used to find out how you are performing.

Feminine hygiene products: maxi pads, sanitary napkins, and tampons used during menstrual cycles.

FICA: 7.5% of your paycheck goes to the Social Security office. Your employer matches that amount. This money comes out of your paycheck each time you are paid. You can request a summary of your social security account from the Social Security office.

Fire department: the local government department responsible for preventing and putting out fires.

Flea market: a big yard sale in a specific location where individual people set up tables in an area to sell their items.

Follow-up question: used to get additional information.

401(k): a pretax retirement plan where you can contribute to a retirement fund by having the money taken out of your paycheck. The name refers to the section of U.S. Tax Code authorizing the plan.

Full-time: employees work up to 40 hours a week and may work overtime.

Gangs: groups of people (usually youths) who stake out territory and rights in an area.

Garage Sale/Yard Sale: a sale held by individuals or neighborhoods in their garages or yards.

General Equivalency Diploma (GED): a certificate documenting your ability to do basic reading, math, problem solving, and communications at the level of a high-school graduate.

General practitioner: a doctor who has general knowledge of medicine and can give care for most common illnesses.

Generic drugs: drugs sold under their chemical name that contain the same active ingredients as brand-name drugs but are less expensive.

Gerontologist: a doctor specializing in the health of the elderly.

Gestures: movements you make with your arms and hands while speaking.

Goal: a skill, event, or object you want to achieve.

Health food store: a specialty shop that focuses on natural healing and health, selling vitamins, herbs, mineral supplements, and wholesome foods.

Hiring agencies: companies that specialize in placing people in jobs.

HMO (Health Maintenance Organization): an HMO is a group of doctors who join together to form an organization.

Homeowner's insurance: coverage against specific loss on your house in return for paying premiums.

Hourly employee: an employee who is paid for each hour and minute they work according to an agreed-upon hourly rate.

HOV (Highly Occupied Vehicle) lane: lane set aside for vehicles containing more than two or three people. Sometimes called "carpool lanes."

Immediate family members: your mother, father, brothers, and sisters.

Immediate relatives of U.S. citizens: parents, spouses, and unmarried children under the age of 21.

Immigrant: in this book, anyone who is coming to live and work in the United States from another country and culture – whether short-term, migrant worker, or permanent resident.

Immigration and Naturalization Services (INS): the part of the U.S. government that controls the immigration process.

Immunization: an injection of medication that helps the body protect itself from diseases.

Infrastructure: the underlying features of the political and social systems that serve the people of an area.

Insurance: a contract with a company to protect you against financial losses if your car is damaged or if you damage someone else's car.

Insurance claim: a formal request for the insurance company to pay for any damages done to your car, or any other cars damaged in an accident.

Insurance policy: a written description of the risks you are insured against and the amounts you and the insurance company agree to pay if an accident occurs.

Insurance premium: the amount of money you pay to the insurance company on a regular basis to keep the insurance coverage active.

Interest: the fee paid to borrow money or an amount that accures to your deposited savings.

Interest rate: the percentage the bank will charge you for borrowing money.

Internal Revenue Service (IRS): the government agency in charge of the collection of taxes.

International calls: calls made to a different country.

Internist: a doctor specializing in the treatment of internal organs.

Interstate calls: calls made to another state.

Interstate highways: roads that cross state borders. Many interstates are also expressways.

Intrastate calls: calls made within your state.

Investment account: an account where you give your money to a bank for them to use and they pay you interest on the money in the account.

Jargon: words that are used by a specific group of people or in a specific work setting.

Junior college: a college offering a two-year program where the coursework can then be transferred to a college or university offering a four-year program.

Khakis: pants in solid colors that are for casual or business casual wear. They are more formal than jeans and less formal than dress pants, and worn by both men and women.

Landlord: the person or company who owns the apartments or rental property.

Learner's permit: allows you to drive a car as long as there is another licensed driver with you.

Leave of absence: an extended period of time during which you do not work.

Life insurance: an optional benefit you may choose to carry that will pay your beneficiaries when you die.

Loan: credit you receive from a bank, credit union, or loan/lending companies.

Local calls: calls within your city or city area.

Long distance: a call made to someone outside your area code.

Mentor: someone you trust who can give you advice on your new experiences.

Monogamous: the practice of being sexually intimate with only one other person.

Monthly charge account: a credit account where whatever money you charge during the month is due at the end of the month.

Mortgage: a long-term home loan. A fixed interest rate mortgage will have the same interest rate for the whole length of the mortgage. A variable interest rate mortgage will have an interest rate that changes, based on the current national interest rate.

Motor Vehicle Department: is a governmental office run by each individual state.

Mouthwash: a liquid rinse used after brushing your teeth that will freshen breath and may kill germs in the mouth.

Moving company: a company hired to move your belongings.

National brands: products sold throughout America under a single company's name.

Naturalization: the process by which U.S. citizenship is granted to a permanent resident.

Non-Prepaid phone card: a card issued by a local or long-distance phone company that allows calls to be billed to the caller's home phone.

Nursing home: a facility that provides living arrangements and care for the elderly, chronically ill, or individuals recovering from surgery or injuries.

Open-ended question: does not invite a particular answer, but allows for discussion.

Ophthalmologists: professionals licensed to do eye surgery in addition to standard eye exams and care.

Optometrists: professionals licensed to do eye exams and prescribe eyeglasses and/or contact lenses.

Oral surgeons: usually have special equipment and facilities for surgical procedures in the mouth.

Orientation: is when they tell you about their company and their policies.

Otolaryngologist/ENT: a doctor specializing in problems with the ear, nose, and throat.

Outlet Mall/Factory Outlet: a large outdoor shopping mall selling merchandise at a discounted price.

Outpatient surgery: a surgery, after which you go home, rather than remaining in the hospital.

Over-the-counter drugs: medicines you can purchase without a doctor's prescription.

Overtime: hours worked more than regularly scheduled hours (typically more than 40 hours a week).

Pager: a small device that can be hooked over a belt or carried in a pocket that allows the wearer to receive a caller's phone number or a short message. Sometimes called a "beeper."

Panty hose: also known as nylons, hose, or stockings that a woman wears over her legs, typically one piece. They range in colors from skin tones to white, navy, and black.

Parolees: aliens who, at the time they apply, are not admissible as non-immigrants or permanent residents.

Part-time: employee usually works less than 35 hours a week.

Pay-per-view: allows you to watch a movie or special for a set fee.

Pediatrician: a doctor specializing in children's health.

Pension plan: a retirement plan consisting of specific amounts of money a company will automatically save for you.

Perk: something extra you get other than your base salary.

Permanent resident card: a document issued to permanent residents. Formerly called an alien registration card. Sometimes known as a "green card."

Personal space: the actual physical space between people.

PIN: Personal Identification Number, a code set by the phone card issuer to allow use of the phone card.

Podiatrist: a doctor specializing in foot problems.

Police department: local government department responsible for maintaining order, enforcing laws, and preventing and detecting crime.

Polo shirt: a collared knit shirt, usually short-sleeved. Many companies will have their logos sewn onto the shirt.

POS (Point of Service): a POS allows you to choose any doctor you want, but generally pays less of the costs than does an HMO or a PPO.

PPO (Preferred Provider Organization): a PPO allows you to choose a doctor from an approved listing of doctors provided by your insurance company.

Pre-approved mortgage: a mortgage you can get before you choose a house. It is set to an amount you can afford.

Pre-approved/Pre-admitted: a non-emergency surgery or hospital stay for which you or your doctor have obtained approval from your insurance company.

Premium channels: feature recently released movies and specials. Premium channels are available at an additional charge.

Prepaid phone card: a card with a set amount of minutes available that is used until it is out of call time.

Preschool: a school-style day care for children typically between the ages of 3 and 6.

Prescription drug card: a card issued by an insurance company which you show at a pharmacy to get a lower cost for prescription drugs.

Prescription drugs: medicines your doctor will tell you to take for specific medical conditions.

Pretax option: your benefits are automatically taken out of your paycheck before taxes are calculated on your income.

Priority date: the date the immigrant visa petition was filed.

Property taxes: the taxes you pay to the government, usually twice a year, for owning a property.

PTO days: paid time off, extra vacation days awarded for achievements like perfect attendance or for length of service.

Racial profiling: the use of distinctive features or characteristics such as race by which prejudgments are made.

Realtor: a person who specializes in helping people find homes.

Reference: a person you know who is willing to talk to employers about you and your work experience. A professional reference is usually someone who can talk about your work experience and professionalism. A personal reference is a friend or mentor who can tell the employer about you.

Referral: when a doctor recommends you visit another doctor, typically a specialist.

Refugees: aliens who apply for and are assigned refugee status before coming to the United States to avoid being persecuted in their home country.

Rent: monthly payment for housing.

Renter's insurance: insures all your property in case of loss or damage, in which event the insurance company would give you money to replace your belongings.

Republic: the people elect representatives to make the laws.

Restroom: toilet facilities.

Resumé: a formal listing of your job experiences and education. In some countries this is called a curriculum vitae.

Retirement: the time when people are older and have finished working.

Retirement home or community: a housing complex where an elderly person who has retired from their life's work may choose to live. Some retirement homes offer on-site nursing as well.

Revolving charge account: a credit account where you need not pay the full amount due, but you are charged interest for any unpaid amount that carries forward to the next month.

Salaried employee: an employee who is paid a fixed rate for each pay period no matter how many hours he/she works during that period.

Sanitary pads: pads made of cotton or other absorbent materials used to control menstruation. They may have a thin plastic layer to prevent leaks. They are made in many different sizes and shapes.

Seasonal workers: typically used only during the season they are needed.

Security deposit: an amount of money, usually the value of one or two months' rent, required by apartment complexes to cover damage you might do to the apartment.

Self-Employment tax: If you are self-employed, you pay a self-employment tax of 15%.

Senior day-care center: a facility with trained staff that assists the elderly or disabled in participation in daily activities outside their home.

Service roads: roads beside an expressway that may be used to exit and enter the expressway.

Sexually transmitted diseases (STDs): diseases people get with unprotected sexual contact.

Shampoo: liquid soap designed for your hair.

Shopping mall: a large group of specialty stores and department stores together in one location.

Sit-down dining: a restaurant where you tell a server what items you want and he or she brings your meal from the kitchen to your table when it is ready. In general, uneaten food may be boxed up for you to take home.

Slang: a casual word or expression.

Social security number: the number of your social security account, used as a means of identification by many organizations, schools, banks, and the government.

Specialist: a doctor who has had additional training in a particular area of medicine.

Specialty store: a store that specializes in a particular product.

Sports jacket: also known as a sports coat, it is a jacket that is not made of the same color and fabric as the trousers/pants. A tie may or may not be required to complete the outfit. (See photo in Business/Formal, page 49.)

State income tax: many states also require you to pay taxes on the money you earn.

Stock options: a benefit where employees are either paid with company stock rather than money or are offered the opportunity to purchase company stock at a reduced price.

Store brands/Generic brands: products that are similar to national brand products, but are sold by each store under its own name (store brands) or no name at all (generic brands).

Strip mall: a small group of specialty stores in a row.

Superintendent: the person who maintains or repairs the rental property.

Supermarket/Grocery store: a store that sells food and household products.

Superstore: a combination of a grocery store and department store.

Surgery: a medical procedure done by a doctor to treat an injury or disease.

Talk radio: radio stations that feature news and discussion programs.

Tampons: small rolls of absorbent material inserted into the vagina to absorb menstrual flow. Most tampons come in applicators to make them easy to insert. Tampons are removed by pulling on the strings attached to the tampon. See usage instructions on tampon packages for more information.

Taxes: extra fees charged on goods and property you buy and the money you earn.

Taxicab: a car you can hire to take you from one place to another.

Technical/Vocational schools: schools that teach skills and provide training for a specific job.

Telemarketers: people whose job is to call people and try to sell them products or services.

Term life insurance: money will only be paid to your beneficiaries if you die while you are paying the policy premiums.

Test drive: an opportunity to drive a car before purchasing it, to check it for any problems and decide if you like the car.

Tipping: giving someone an additional amount of money, called a "tip" or "gratuity," for service they have provided or for doing an exceptional job.

Toilet paper: thin, absorbent paper usually in a roll. Toilet paper is used to clean yourself after a bowel movement or urination.

Toll free: phone numbers with an area code of 800, 888, 877, and 866 are paid by the owner of the number.

Toll roads: roads that require you to pay a fee after you have traveled a certain number of miles and before you exit the road. Toll bridges and toll tunnels require you to pay to cross over or go through.

Toothpaste: a cleaner used on a brush to clean teeth.

Transcript: a list of the courses you have taken and the grade you received in other schools.

Undocumented immigrants: more often referred to as illegal immigrants—they do not have permission to live or work in the United States.

Unit price: the price of a product based on the weight or quantity purchased.

Urinals: wall-mounted ceramic basins flushed with water that men use while standing up to urinate.

Utilities: the services of electricity, natural gas, water, and sewage.

Vaccination: an injection of medication that helps the body protect itself from diseases.

Vesting schedule: a plan that requires you to work for a company for a certain number of years before you can fully use any money the company has contributed to your 401(k) or pension plan.

Vocabulary: the number of words you know.

Volatility: how risky an investment is.

Warranty: a guarantee by the company to repair or replace defective items for a certain period of time after purchase.

Wholesale club: a members-only club located in a large warehouse featuring bulk (large-sized) quantities of products at a discounted price.

Work ethic: a person's set of values based on the belief in hard work and effort.

W-2 statement: lists how much you earned in the previous year and how much tax you paid.

APPENDIX A

Vocabulary to Know

Chapter 1—Only in America

Words and Phrases to Know: Fill out this work sheet for common words or phrases and questions you may use when you are trying to understand America and all it has to offer. You should use a dictionary that translates the English language to your language, or you can use the Internet (for example: http://world.altavista.com/) to help you complete this exercise. Translate the words and phrases from the left column into your language and write the translation in the right column.

English Term or Phrase	Your Language Term
American values	
United States culture	
Freedom	
Lifestyle choices	
American infrastructure	
Republic	
American workplace skills	
Work ethics	
Job skills	
Terrorism	

Chapter 2—Here to Stay! Immigration and Citizenship

Words and Phrases to Know: Fill out this work sheet for common words or phrases and questions you may use when seeking naturalization or citizenship. You should use a dictionary that translates the English language to your language, or you can use the Internet (for example: http://world.altavista.com/) to help you complete this exercise. Translate the words and phrases from the left column into your language and write the translation in the right column.

English Term or Phrase	Your Language Term
Immigration and Naturalization Services (INS)	
Where is the local INS department?	
What are the different ways to become an American citizen?	
What forms do I need to fill out?	
Social security number	
Where is the social security office?	
How long will this take?	
Does this expire?	
How do I help my family get green cards?	

Chapter 3—Learning the Language

Words and Phrases to Know: Fill out this work sheet for common words or phrases you may use when learning the American English language. You should use a dictionary that translates the English language to your language, or you can use the Internet (for example: http://world.altavista.com/) to help you complete this exercise. Translate the words and phrases from the left column into your language and write the translation in the right column.

English Term or Phrase	**Your Language Term**
Where can I take classes on American English?	
I do not understand what that means.	
Jargon	
Slang	
What does that body movement mean?	
Gestures	
Where is the nearest library?	
Could you please say that again?	
You are standing too close to me.	

Chapter 4—Hygiene, Grooming, and Clothing

Words and Phrases to Know: Fill out this work sheet for common words and phrases you may use for hygiene, grooming, and clothing. You should use a dictionary that translates the English language to your language, or you can use the Internet (for example: http://world.altavista.com/) to help you complete this exercise. Translate the words and phrases from the left column into your language and write the translation in the right column.

English Term or Phrase	Your Language Term
Where is the restroom?	
What is this product used for?	
Sanitary pad and tampon	
Condom	
Soap	
Shampoo and conditioner	
Deodorant and antiperspirant	
Toothpaste and mouthwash	
What is the acceptable clothing for this event?	
Jewelry	
Shoes	
Where is the nearest laundry or dry cleaner?	
Haircut	

Chapter 5—Cash and Credit

Words and Phrases to Know: Fill out this work sheet for common words and phrases you may use when learning about American currency, credit, and banking. You should use a dictionary that translates the English language to your language, or you can use the Internet (for example: http://world.altavista.com/) to help you complete this exercise. Translate the words and phrases from the left column into your language and write the translation in the right column.

English Term or Phrase	Your Language Term
Cash	
Personal check	
Credit card	
Debit card	
Automatic teller machine	
Cash a check	
To endorse	
Payment	
Payee	
Savings account	
Checking account	
Wiring money	
Withdrawal	
How much does it cost?	
What forms of payment do you accept?	
When is the bill payment due?	
I need to take out a loan.	
Interest rate	
What credit card do you take?	

Chapter 6—Housing

Words and Phrases to Know: Fill out this work sheet for common words and phrases you may use about housing. You should use a dictionary that translates the English language to your language, or you can use the Internet (for example: http://world.altavista.com/) to help you complete this exercise. Translate the words and phrases from the left column into your language and write the translation in the right column.

English Term or Phrase	Your Language Term
Apartment	
Renting	
Renter's insurance	
Equity	
Mortgage	
Realtor	
How can I find the right home?	
What should I look for when buying a home?	
Mortgage	
Closing costs	
Homeowner's insurance	
Property taxes	
Moving services	
Where is the post office?	
What is the postage rate for this package?	
How do I change to a new address?	
Postage stamps	
Post office box	

Chapter 7—Transportation

Words and Phrases to Know: Fill out this work sheet for common words and phrases you may use when you need transportation. You should use a dictionary that translates the English language to your language, or you can use the Internet (for example: http://world.altavista.com/) to help you complete this exercise. Translate the words and phrases from the left column into your language and write the translation in the right column.

English Term or Phrase	Your Language Term
Where is the...	
Bus station	
Train station	
Subway	
Taxi stand	
Schedule	
Fare	
Where is the Department of Motor Vehicles?	
Driving lessons	
Driving tests	
Driver's license	
Car dealership	
New car	
Used car	
Renting a car	
Test drive	
How do I get automobile insurance?	
Where is the closest service station?	

Chapter 8—Shopping

Words and Phrases to Know: Fill out this work sheet for common words and phrases you may use when you are shopping. You should use a dictionary that translates the English language to your language, or you can use the Internet (for example: http://world.altavista.com/) to help you complete this exercise. Translate the words and phrases from the left column into your language and write the translation in the right column.

English Term or Phrase	Your Language Term
Where is the…	
Where can I buy…	
Supermarket or grocery store	
Department store	
Convenience store	
Drugstore or pharmacy	
Shopping mall	
Factory outlet	
How much does this cost?	
Do you have this in my size?	
Can you help me find…	
Exchange rate	
Sales tax	
On sale	
Coupons	
Where is the fitting room?	

Vocabulary to Know

Chapter 9—Dining In, Dining Out

Words and Phrases to Know: Fill out this work sheet for common words and phrases you may use when buying food, eating out, or dining in. You should use a dictionary that translates the English language to your language, or you can use the Internet (for example: http://world.altavista.com/) to help you complete this exercise. Translate the words and phrases from the left column into your language and write the translation in the right column.

English Term or Phrase	Your Language Term
I would like…	
May I order…	
Could I get the check please?	
Meat	
Fish	
Pasta	
Fruit	
Vegetable	
Starch	
Beverages or drinks	
Appetizer	
Soup	
Salad	
Entrée	
Dessert	
Is it proper to…	
Please pass me the…	

Chapter 10—Out on Your Own

Words and Phrases to Know: Fill out this work sheet for common words and phrases you may use for your living arrangements or moving out on your own. You should use a dictionary that translates the English language to your language, or you can use the Internet (for example: http://world.altavista.com/) to help you complete this exercise. Translate the words and phrases from the left column into your language and write the translation in the right column.

English Term or Phrase	Your Language Term
How long should I plan to stay with you?	
What can I do to help around the home?	
Can you help me to...	
I will pay for...	
Goals	
Planning	
Realtor	
Rent	
Mortgage	
Utilities	
Telephone service	
Cable television service	
Insurance	
Bill due date	
Meeting new people:	
Hello, my name is...	
Where are you from?	
What do you do?	
Do you enjoy...	

Chapter 11—Balancing Home and Work

Words and Phrases to Know: Fill out this work sheet for common words and phrases you may use for balancing your life. You should use a dictionary that translates the English language to your language, or you can use the Internet (for example: http://world.altavista.com/) to help you complete this exercise. Translate the words and phrases from the left column into your language and write the translation in the right column.

English Term or Phrase	Your Language Term
Extended family	
Day care	
Preschool	
Nursing home	
Retirement home	
Health	
Where is the closest hospital?	
Do you know of a good…	
Doctor	
Dentist	
Clinic	
Do I need to schedule an appointment?	
Medical insurance	
Co-pay	
Prescription	
Over-the-counter	
Shot or immunization	
National holiday	
Where is the public library?	
How do I contact the police?	

Chapter 12—Education

Words and Phrases to Know: Fill out this work sheet for common words and phrases you may use when searching for educational options. You should use a dictionary that translates the English language to your language, or you can use the Internet (for example: http://world.altavista.com/) to help you complete this exercise. Translate the words and phrases from the left column into your language and write the translation in the right column.

English Term or Phrase	Your Language Term
How do I transfer my credits?	
Transcript	
Certification	
Seminar or workshop	
How do I enroll my child in school?	
How does the grading system work?	
Grammar school	
Middle school	
High school	
College	
University	
Diploma	
College degree	
Advanced degree	

Chapter 13—Getting a Job and Keeping a Job

Words and Phrases to Know: Fill out this work sheet for common words and phrases you may use when searching for a job. You should use a dictionary that translates the English language to your language, or you can use the Internet (for example: http://world.altavista.com/) to help you complete this exercise. Translate the words and phrases from the left column into your language and write the translation in the right column.

English Term or Phrase	Your Language Term
Classified ads	
Networking	
Help Wanted	
Resumé	
References	
Work samples	
How do I apply?	
What position are you trying to fill?	
Application	
Interview	
When will I find out if I have the job?	
What will the rate of pay be?	
Salary	
Wage	
Benefits	
What is my work schedule?	
Is there a proper uniform?	
How long will the training be?	
What is the policy on…?	

Chapter 14—Taxes and On-the-Job Benefits

Words and Phrases to Know: Fill out this work sheet for common words and phrases you may use when discussing job benefits. You should use a dictionary that translates the English language to your language, or you can use the Internet (for example: http://world.altavista.com/) to help you complete this exercise. Translate the words and phrases from the left column into your language and write the translation in the right column.

English Term or Phrase	Your Language Term
Where is the Internal Revenue Department?	
Taxes	
What is the local sales tax?	
Pretax options	
Which benefits do I pay for?	
Are the benefits optional?	
Do I need to fill out any forms?	
Life insurance	
Health insurance	
Deductible	
Prescription drug card	
Vision coverage	
Dental coverage	
Retirement plans	
Paid time off	
Absence	

Chapter 15—Communication at Work

Words and Phrases to Know: Fill out this work sheet for common words and phrases you may use when communicating at work. You should use a dictionary that translates the English language to your language, or you can use the Internet (for example: http://world.altavista.com/) to help you complete this exercise. Translate the words and phrases from the left column into your language and write the translation in the right column.

English Term or Phrase	Your Language Term
Can I schedule an appointment to see you?	
I have a problem.	
It upsets me when you...	
Hello, how are you today?	
May I help you?	
Have a good day.	
Please	
Thank you	
Will you get me...	

Chapter 16—Telephones and Other Technology

Words and Phrases to Know: Fill out this work sheet for common words and phrases you may use regarding telephones and technology. You should use a dictionary that translates the English language to your language, or you can use the Internet (for example: http://world.altavista.com/) to help you complete this exercise. Translate the words and phrases from the left column into your language and write the translation in the right column.

English Term or Phrase	Your Language Term
Telephone	
Local phone service	
Long-distance service	
International phone service	
What are your rates?	
How do I make an international phone call?	
Toll free	
Collect call	
Deposit	
Could you give me the phone number for...	
Could you direct me to the nearest pay phone?	
Cellular phone	
Pager	
Facsimile machine	

Chapter 17—Mass Communication

Words and Phrases to Know: Fill out this work sheet for common words and phrases you may use regarding the media. You should use a dictionary that translates the English language to your language, or you can use the Internet (for example: http://world.altavista.com/) to help you complete this exercise. Translate the words and phrases from the left column into your language and write the translation in the right column.

English Term or Phrase	Your Language Term
Television	
Program	
What time is the program on?	
Networks	
Cable television	
How do I get cable television?	
Radio	
Music	
News	
What is a good radio station?	
Newspapers	
Magazines	
The Internet	

Chapter 18—Finding and Being a Mentor

Words and Phrases to Know: Fill out this work sheet for common words and phrases about mentors and mentoring. You should use a dictionary that translates the English language to your language, or you can use the Internet (for example: http://world.altavista.com/) to help you complete this exercise. Translate the words and phrases from the left column into your language and write the translation in the right column.

English Term or Phrase	Your Language Term
Mentor	
Friend	
Family	
Could you show me…	
Will you help me…	
What is…	
Where are…	
How do you…	

Vocabulary to Know

Common Words

Days of the Week	Your Language	Months of the Year	Your Language
Monday		January	
Tuesday		February	
Wednesday		March	
Thursday		April	
Friday		May	
Saturday		June	
Sunday		July	
		August	
Weekday		September	
Weekend		October	
Work week		November	
		December	

Common Words

Times of the Day	Your Language	Seasons	Your Language
Seconds		Winter	
Minutes		Spring	
Hours		Summer	
Morning (a.m.)		Fall	
Afternoon			
Evening (p.m.)			

Common Words

Weather	Your Language	Colors	Your Language
Cold		Black	
Cool		Blue	
Hot		Brown	
Warm		Green	
Sunny		Orange	
Cloudy		Pink	
Rainy		Purple	
Snowy		Red	
Degrees		Yellow	
Humid		White	
Storm		Dark in color	
Blizzard		Light in color	

APPENDIX B

Student Visas Are Not All the Same!

So you are going to, or are in, the United States to get an education. You need to be aware that all student visas are not the same. Some will allow you to work on campus (only for the school) and others will allow you to work off campus (for anyone). Use this chart to help you better understand your work eligibility. This is basic information regarding student visas. Talk to your foreign student advisor or visit on of the websites listed below for more detailed information.

Visa Type	Work Eligibility

F-1 Student Visa	**Prior to being granted this visa you:**
	✦ Must demonstrate sufficient funds for all tuition and living costs for the first year of study in the U.S.
	During the first year of study you:
	✦ May not work off campus
	✦ May have an on-campus job limited to 20 hours per week (provided it does not displace a U.S. resident).
	After the first year of study:
	✦ The student may ask the INS for permission to accept off-campus employment.
	✦ This is usually granted if:
	  ▪ Student is in good academic standing
	  ▪ Student is experiencing financial hardship through no fault of his/her own.
	Permission is typically valid for one year after it is granted.

M-1 **Vocational Student Visa**	**Prior to being granted this visa you:** ✦ Must demonstrate sufficient funds for all tuition and living costs for your entire stay in the U.S. **During the entire stay in the U.S.:** ✦ The student may not accept any form of employment, except: ▪ they may be granted one period of *Employment for Practical Training* for a period of time equal to one month for each four months of full course of study, not to exceed 6 months.
J-1 **Exchange Visitor Visa**	**Prior to being granted this visa you:** ✦ Must demonstrate sufficient funds for all tuition and living costs for your entire stay in the U.S. **During the entire stay in the U.S.:** ✦ The student is limited on campus employment to 20 hours per week while school is in session, 40 hours otherwise. ✦ You may not accept off campus employment without authorization from INS.
B-2 **Tourist Visa**	✦ The B-2 visa is not considered a student visa. ✦ If you study in the U.S. on a B-2 visa, you could be deported. ✦ If you choose to get a B-2 visa to investigate schools and think that you may later want to switch to an F-1 or J-1 visa, get a "Prospective Student" stamp on it.

While here on a student visa, you may be required to check in with your foreign student advisor and the INS. Additional resources you may find helpful include:

✦ www.eduPASS.org
✦ www.travel.state.gov
✦ www.ins.usdoj.gov
✦ www.usgreencard.com

Index

Numerics

401(k) 171, 205
911 128

A

accredited 142, 147, 205
act of expatriation 20
alien 12, 22, 205
America 5
    hopes and dreams 5
American ways 3
American workplace 1
American workplace, job, skills 6
    look at your skills 6
    work ethics 6
antiperspirant 41, 50, 205
assisted living 121
    facility 137, 205
associate degree 147, 205
asylees 22, 205
ATM (Automatic Teller Machine) 54, 61, 205
    card 55, 61, 205
auto loans 81, 85, 205

B

baby changing stations 39, 50, 205
bachelor's degree 147, 205
bank 54–58
    accounts 54
    cashing your check 58
    certificate of deposit (CD) 56, 62, 206
    checking accounts 55
    depositing money 57
    loan 56
    mortgages 57
    retirement accounts 57
    savings account 56, 62
    services 54
barcode 95, 100, 205

becoming a U.S. citizen - see naturalization
beneficiaries 171, 205
benefits 163, 165, 171, 205
    additional 169–170
        Family Medical Leave Act 170
        funeral (bereavement) leave 170
        holidays 169
        leaves of absence 170
        long-term leave of absence 170
        paid time off 169
        sick days 169
        vacation days 169
    extra features 165
    health benefits 165
    pretax option 165
    savings plan 165
    when do you pay 165
boarding schools 143
budget 116, 117
buffet 110, 206
bureau of motor vehicles
    photo ID 79
business casual 50, 206
business casual clothing 48
business/ formal clothing 47
buying a house 66–70
    closing costs 69
    homeowner's insurance 69
    inspection 68
    mortgage 69
    property taxes 69
    selecting a house 68

C

cable TV 198, 206
cafeteria 110, 206
campground 136, 137, 206
car accident 82
cash 61, 206
cash - see currency
cashing a check 62, 206
casual clothing 47
catalog 100, 206
cell phone 189, 206
ceremony to take the oath 19
certification 142, 147, 206
chain restaurants 137, 138, 206
change-of-address form 72
check 55, 62, 206
checking account 62, 206

Christmas 131
citizen 22, 206
citizenship 11
claim 82
clean body 8
clinic 123, 138, 206
closed-ended question 179, 207
closing 69, 73, 206
closing costs 69, 73, 207
clothing 35, 45
    care 46
    dressing for the job 45
    inappropriate clothing 45
    interviewing 46
    shoes 48
collect call 189, 207
communicate 8, 25
communication 173, 179, 207
communication at work 173–178
    cell phones 188
    communicate with your boss 175
    electronic communication 178
        e-mail 178
    listening 173
        check if you understood 173
    pagers 188
    resolving conflict 176
    speaking 174
    talking to the customer 177
    talking to your co-workers 176
    telephones 188
    use questions to manage workplace communication 174
    written communication 175
company culture 161, 207
conditioner 40, 50, 207
condom 39, 50, 207
conflict 179, 207
consumers 87, 100, 207
continuing education classes 142, 147, 207
convenience store 100, 207
conventional mortgage 69, 74, 207
converter box 193, 198, 207
co-pay 138, 171, 207
county 9, 207
coupon 100, 207
cover letter 154, 161, 207

credit card 58–60, 207
    credit card 62
    credit rating 58, 62
    managing 60
        missing a payment 60
        stolen credit cards 60
    Master Card 59
    monthly charge accounts 59
    platinum 60
    revolving charge accounts 59
    secure 60
    store 59
    types of credit cards 59
    Visa 59
credit rating 207
crime 128
currency 53
curriculum vitae 154

D

dandruff 40, 50, 208
day care 138, 208
debit card 55, 62, 208
decisions, making your own 114–116
    getting a plan 115
    getting what you need 115
    setting goals 114
deductible 171, 208
defending yourself 128
delivery 208
dental floss 42, 50, 208
deodorant 41, 50, 208
department store 100, 208
deposit 182, 189, 208
destination sign 85, 208
dining 103
dining out 105–108
    restaurants, types of 106
        buffet 106
        cafeteria 106
        delivery 106
        fast-food 106
        sit-down dining 106
    the American restaurant experience 107
        appetizers 107
        dessert 107
        drinks 107

Index

entrée 107
soup/salad 107
tipping 107
direct deposit 57, 171, 208
discount store 101, 208
discounted rates 136
discrimination 9, 208
documents needed to work
    social security card 20
documents needed to work in the U.S. 20
dollar 53, 62, 208
down payment 67, 74, 208
dress shoes 50, 208
driver's license 78
driving a car 78–80
    getting a driver's license 78
        driving lessons 79
        driving test 79
        learning permit 79, 86, 212
driving on the road 83–84
    county roads 83
    exits 84
    expressways 83
    interstates 83
    lanes 84
    state roads 83
    toll bridges 83
    toll roads 83
    toll tunnels 83
    town and city streets 83
drugstore 101, 208
dry cleaning 46, 50, 208
drying your hands 38

E

eating with other people 108–110
    family style 109
    manners 108
education 141
    advanced 145–147
        associate degree 146
        bachelor's degree 145
        technical colleges 147
    expanding your 141–143
        individual classes 142
        professional certifications 142
        seminars and workshops 143

        transferring your education 142
    system 143–145
        GED 145
        grade levels 144
        private schools 143
        public schools 143
electronic communication 179, 208
emergencies 128
emergency medical team (EMT) 129, 138
emergency room (ER) 124, 138, 208
emissions test 85, 209
employee pool 156, 161, 209
English 8
ENT
    ear, nose and throat 123
equity 66, 74, 209
escrow account 70, 74, 209
ESL 34, 209
ethnic restaurants 106
exact change 76, 85, 209
exchange rate 93, 101, 209
exits 84, 85, 209
express lane 84, 85, 209
expressways 85, 209
extended family 119, 138, 209

F

fact-finding question 179, 209
factory outlet 101, 213
Family Medical Leave (FML) 171, 209
family style eating 209
family, taking care of 119–122
    after school programs 121
    care of the elderly 121
    childcare 120
    daycare 120
    preschool 121
    when someone is sick 122
fare box 85, 209
farmer's market 101, 209
fast-food 110, 209
fax machine 187, 189, 209
FDIC 54
federal U.S. holidays 129
feedback question 179, 209
feminine hygiene 39
    products 37, 50, 210

filling out a job application 153
fingerprinted 18
fire department 129, 138, 210
firearms 128
flea market 101, 210
FML - see family medical leave act
follow-up question 179, 210
freedom of America 3
    employment 4
    government 4
    infrastructure 4
    lifestyle 3
    religion 3
fruit salad 2
full time 210
full time employees 156
full-time employees 161

G

gangs 128, 138
garage sale 101, 210
GED 147, 210
General Equivalency Diploma - see GED
general practitioner (GP) 123, 138, 210
generic brands 95, 101, 217
generic drugs 171, 210
gerontologist 123, 138, 210
gestures 34, 210
goal 114, 117, 210
grading scale 144
grocery shopping 103–105
    ethnic groceries 103
    fruits & vegetables 104
    health food 104
    meat, poultry & fish 104
    pre-packaged foods 105
grocery store 101, 217
grooming 35, 43
    body piercing 44
    employer regulations 44
    hair 43
    jewelry 43
    tattoos 45
guns 128

H

health benefits 166–167
dental coverage 167
elective insurance 167
health insurance 166
    co-pay 166
    deductible 166
    generic drugs 167
    HMO 166
    PPO 166
    prescription drug card 167
    referral 166
vision coverage 167
health food store 110, 210
Health Maintenance Organization - see HMO
high school equivalent - see GED
hiring agencies 161, 210
HMO (Health Maintenance Organization) 171, 210
holiday
    gift giving 133
    religious 132
    saying Thank You 133
    special events 132
holidays 129–133
homeowner's insurance 210
hourly employee 155, 161, 211
housing 63
housing options 63–64
    apartment 63
    condominium 64
    house 63
HOV (Highly Occupied Vehicle) 84
    lane 85, 211
hygiene 35
    after bathing 41
    bathing / showering 40
    body hair 41
    body hair for men 42
    body hair for women 41
    hands and fingernails 41
    keeping clean 40
    mouth care 42
    perfume and cologne 41
    washing your hair 40

I

illegal aliens 12, 15
immediate relatives of U.S. citizens 22, 211

immigrant 2, 9, 211
    undocumented 23, 218
immigration 11
Immigration and Naturalization Services (INS)
    22, 211
immunization 138, 211
infrastructure 9, 211
INS 11–21, 22, 211
insurance 85, 211
insurance claim 85, 211
insurance policy 86, 211
insurance premium 86, 211
interest 56, 62, 211
interest rate 56, 62, 211
Internal Revenue Service (IRS) 171
international calls 183, 189, 211
internet 197–198
    browsers 197
    search engines 197
internist 123, 138, 211
interstate calls 183, 189, 211
interstate highways 86, 211
interview, getting ready 153
    questions 153
interviewing for a job 154–155
    during the interview 155
    starting the interview 154
intrastate calls 183, 189, 212
investment 56
investment account 62, 212
IRS 163, 171, 211

J

jargon 34, 212
job application process 152
    documentation 152
    references 152
    work samples 152
job openings, finding 150–151
    cable TV 151
    flyers 151
    help wanted signs 150
    hiring agencies 151
    internet 151
    network 150
    newspapers 150
    radio stations 151
    walk in 151
job, looking for a 149
junior college 145, 147, 212

K

khakis 50, 212

L

landlord 64, 74, 212
language, learning the 25–27
    computer programs and the internet 27
    go to a class 26
    on the job 26
    teach yourself 26
leave of absence 171, 212
life insurance 171, 212
loan 62, 212
local calls 189, 212
local transportation 75–78
    bus 75
        how to ride 76
            destination sign 76
            fare box 76
    commuter trains 76
    subway 76
        how to ride 77
    taxi 77
long-distance 212

M

magazines 196
media 191
medical care 122–127
    clinics and walk-in doctors 123
    co-pay 124
    dentist 125
    doctor's office 122
    eye care 125
    hospital/ emergency room 124
    immunizations 126
    natural remedies 127
    outpatient surgery 124
    over-the-counter drugs 127
    pre-approval 124
    prescription drugs 125
    preventative drugs 126
    surgery 124
melting pot 2

mentor 8, 117, 199–201, 212
    agreements 111–113
        expenses 113
        how long to stay 112
        paying your way 113
    family member as a mentor 201
    rules for the mentor/immigrant relationship 200
    small groups and organizations 201
mentoring activities 202–203
    communication 202
    daily life 202
    food 203
    fun 203
    money 202
    shopping 203
    socializing 202
    transportation 203
    travel 203
microwave 105
monogamous 50, 212
montessori schools 143
monthly charge account 62, 212
mortgage 62, 66, 74, 212
motor vehicle department 78, 86, 212
mouthwash 42, 50, 212
moving company 74, 212
moving out on your own 116
    affording it 116

N

national brands 95, 101, 213
naturalization 18, 22, 213
    losing your citizenship 20
    the process 18
    the process the oath 19
    the processing the application 19
new home, getting settled 70–73
    appliances 72
    cable television 71
    electric power 70
    garbage removal 71
    getting your mail 72
    homeowner's association dues 71
    moving in 73
    newspaper delivery 71
    telephone 71
    utilities 70
New Year's Day 130
newspapers 196
non-prepaid phone card 189, 213
non-verbal communication 30–33
    body movement and posture 31
    clothing 33
    facial expressions and eye contact 32
    gestures 31
    space 31
    touch 33
    using your voice 32
nursing home 121, 138, 213
nylons - see panty hose

O

open-ended question 179, 213
ophthalmologists 126, 138, 213
opportunities 1
optometrists 125, 138, 213
oral surgeons 125, 138, 213
orientation 157, 161, 213
otolaryngologist/ENT 138, 213
outlet mall 101, 213
outpatient surgery 138, 213
overcoming culture 7
    terrorism 7
over-the-counter drugs 139, 213
overtime 156, 157, 161, 213
owning a car 80–83
    auto insurance 81
    buying a car 80
        compare prices 80
        test drive 81
    caring for 83
    emission test 83
    financing the car 81
    license plates 82

P

pager 186, 189, 213
panty hose 50, 213
parochial schools 143
parolees 23, 213
part-time 214
    161
part-time employee 156

pay-per-view 193, 198, 214
pediatrician 123, 139, 214
pension plan 172, 214
perk 214
permanent resident card 12, 23, 214
permanent resident, applying 15–18
    health issues 17
    visa number 16
Personal Identification Number - see PIN
personal reference 152
personal services 49
personal space 34, 214
pharmacy 101, 208
physically disabled access 38
PIN 189, 214
place setting 106
podiatrist 123, 139, 214
police department 128, 139
polo shirt 47, 50, 214
POS (Point of Service) 172
post office box 73
PPO 172, 214
pre-admitted 124
pre-approved mortgage 69, 74, 214
pre-approved/pre-admitted 139, 214
Preferred Provider Organization -see PPO
premium channels 193, 198, 214
premiums 82
prepaid phone card 189, 214
preschool 139, 214
prescription drug card 172, 214
prescription drugs 139, 215
pretax option 172, 215
pretax programs 168
priority date 16, 23, 215
professional reference 152
property taxes 74, 215
PTO days 172, 215
public restrooms 36

R

racial profiling 7, 9, 215
radio 195
realtor 67, 74, 215
reference 161, 215
referral 172, 215
refugees 23, 215

registry of motor vehicles 78
renouncing your U.S. citizenship 20
rent 65, 74, 215
renting 64–66
    renter's insurance 66, 215
    renters insurance 74
    things to look for 65
        appliances 65
        inspect the apartment first 65
        services 66
        utilities 65
republic 9, 215
restaurants 106
restroom 36, 215
resume 154, 161, 215
retirement 57, 62, 215
retirement home or community 121, 139, 215
revolving charge account 62, 215
rules for success 8

S

safer sex 39
safety and security 127–129
salaried employee 155, 161, 216
sanitary pads 39, 51, 216
sanitation and hygiene 36
savings plans 168–169
    pension plans 168
    stock options 169
seasonal workers 156, 161, 216
security deposit 65, 74, 216
senior citizens 139
senior day-care center 121, 139, 216
September 11, 2001 134
service roads 84, 86, 216
service stations 83
setting career goals 115
sexually transmitted diseases 39, 51, 216
shampoo 40, 51, 216
shop
    where to 87–93
        convenience store 89
        department store 88
        discount store 89
        drugstore 89
        factory outlets 92
        farmer's market 92

flea market 93
garage sale 92
grocery store 87
mall 91
outlets 92
pharmacy 89
shopping mall 91
specialty stores 90
strip mall 91
supermarket 87
superstore 88
wholesale club 90
yard sale 92
shopping basics 93–97
    bar coding 95
    barter 94
    brand-name products 95
    catalogs 97
    comparison shopping 94
    coupons 96
    pricing 95
    sales 95
    sales tax 94
    tipping 96
    value of your money 93
shopping mall 101, 216
shopping, clothes 97–100
    clothing size chart 98
        children's clothing 100
        men 99
        women's clothing 98
sit-down dining 110, 216
slang 34, 216
social organizations 201
social security number 20, 23, 216
socializing 113–114
    religious 113
    social groups 113
speak the language 8
specialist 216
    139
specialty store 101, 216
sports jacket 51, 216
stamps 73
state department 16
STDs 39, 51, 216
stock options 172, 217

store brand 95, 101, 217
strip mall 101, 217
superintendent 64, 74, 217
supermarket 101, 217
superstore 101, 217
surgery 139, 217

T

talk radio 195, 198, 217
tampons 39, 51, 217
taxes 163–164, 217
    types of taxes 164
        federal income tax 164, 171, 210
        FICA 164, 171, 210
        local income tax 164, 172
        self-employment tax 164, 172
        state income tax 164, 172, 216
taxicab 77, 86, 217
technical/vocational schools 147, 217
telemarketers 185, 189, 217
telephones 181–186
    900 numbers 185
    billing 183
    cellular phones 186
    dial 10-10-xxx 184
    directory assistance 185
    international calling 183
    local phone company 181
    long-distance phone service 183
    pay phones 185
    phone basics 182
        collect call 182
        local calls 182
        long-distance 182
        toll free 182
    phone cards 184
        non-prepaid cards 184
        prepaid cards 184
    telephone solicitation 185
television (TV) 191–194
    access 192
    cable TV 193
    network programming 192
        television programs 194–195
    game shows 195
    news programs 194
    talk shows 194

Index

tennis shoes 49
term life insurance 172, 217
test drive 86, 217
thank you note 155
Thanksgiving day 131
tip table 108
tipping 101, 110, 217
toilet facilities 36
toilet paper 37, 51, 217
toilets 36
toll roads 86, 218
toothpaste 42, 51, 218
transcript 142, 148, 218
transportation 75
types of immigrants 12–15
    asylees and refugees 14
    business travel 13
    changing your status 14
    conditions and restrictions 14
    eligibility 14
    green card holders 12
    maintaining your residence 13
    non-immigrants 13
    permanent residents 12
    travel outside the United States 12
    types of documentation 14

U

U.S. citizen 12
U.S. Postal Service 72
understanding American language 27–30
    American English 27
    jargon 29
    listening 30
    slang 28
    speaking the language 30
understanding time 129
undocumented immigrants 12
undocumented immigrants - see illegal alien
uniforms 46
unit price 94, 101
urinals 37, 51, 218
utilities 74, 218

V

vacationing 133–137
    air travel 134
    bus travel 135
    camping 136
    car travel 135
    convention and visitor's bureaus 136
    eating out 137
    identification 137
    laws of the road 135
    lodging 136
    road safety 135
    train travel 134
vaccination 17, 23, 218
vesting schedule 168, 172, 218
visa
    employment-based 16
    family-based 15
vocabulary 34, 218
volatility 62, 218

W

W-2 statement 164, 172, 218
wages/benefits 155–156
    benefits 156
    pay periods 156
warranty 218
washing your hands 37
wholesale club 101, 218
wire-transfers 55
work ethic 218
work history 154
workplace guidelines 156–160
    attitude 158
    breaks 157
    calling off 158
    coming in late 157
    company culture 158
    company policies 160
    diversity
        cultural differences 159
        personal values 159
        religious values 159
        women in the workplace 159
    diversity in the American workplace 159
    finding a substitute 158
    lunch hour 157
    smoking 160
    timeliness 157
    training 158

working overtime 157
your first day 157

Y

yard sale 101, 210

VIDEOS

THE IMMIGRANT'S GUIDE TO THE AMERICAN WORKPLACE VIDEO SERIES

This new video series is designed to help immigrants' transition into the American workplace and develop confidence with the social and cultural settings in America. This series is perfect for line-level service people as well as beginning professionals; anyone who wants to be successful in the U.S. job market. Each video features expert interviews, immigrant interviews, tips and challenges for the transition, and training moments. This series of seven videos is available as a set at $595 or individually at $99. **Buy the complete seven tape set and save!**

#1 - **The Freedom of America**— provides an overview of life and culture in the United States.

#2 - **Neat, Clean, and Orderly**— gives guidelines on grooming, hygiene, and dress on the job.

#3 - **Communication with the World**— provides tips and advice on ways to communicate in the workplace.

#4 - **Professional on the Job**— looks at life on the job, employer expectations, and ways to advance in your career.

#5 - **Culture Shock**— takes a look at all the choices we have, the diversity of America, cultural values, and the media and its impact on our society.

#6 – **Finding a Mentor**— will assist you in finding a mentor, setting up the ground rules to live by, and exploring the role of the mentor.

#7 - **Getting a Job**— focuses on getting yourself ready for the job market, where to find a job, how to create your job resumé, how to apply for a job, and how to get the job.

LEARN FROM THE EXPERTS AND AUTHORS!

TO ORDER:

Call Toll-Free **1-866-332-5905**

Fax your order to **1-317-598-0816**

Online: **http://learnovation.com**

Mail orders to:

Learnovation®, LLC
10831 Thistle Ridge
Fishers, IN 46038-2254

Shipping for $0 to $99 - add 7%
$100 and over - add 6%

Indiana State Residents: please add 5% sales tax

From Najor Educational Publishing, in partnership with Learnovation®, LLC